Leave the Mud Learn to Soar

Leave the Mud Learn to Soar

Elaine Martens Hamilton

Leave the Mud, Learn to Soar
Copyright © 2000 Elaine Martens Hamilton

Discovery House Publishers is affiliated with RBC Ministries, Grand Rapids, Michigan 49512

Discovery House books are distributed to the trade exclusively by Barbour Publishing, Inc., Ulrichsville, Ohio 44683

Unless indicated otherwise, Scripture is taken from the HOLY BIBLE, NEW INTERNATIONAL VERSION. Copyright © 1973, 1978, 1984, by the International Bible Society. Used by permission of Zondervan Bible Publishers.

Some of the information in chapter six is based on material from Dr. Bill and Kristie Gaultiere and is used with their permission. The questions are in their original form. The chart and descriptions have been adapted to reflect the responses of women who have worked through the material with me. For tapes or other written material by Dr. Gaultiere, write to him at 4000 Barranca Parkway, Suite 250, Irvine, California 92604.

Library of Congress Cataloging-in-Publication Data

Hamilton, Elaine Martens
   Leave the Mud, Learn to Soar / by Elaine Martens Hamilton.
      p. cm.
   Includes bibliographical references.
   ISBN 1-57293-062-4
   1. Christian women -- Religious life. I. Title.
BV4527 .H35 2000
248.8'4--dc21   00-029457

Printed in the United States of America
00 01 02 03 04 05 06 07 08 09 10 / CHG / 10 9 8 7 6 5 4 3 2 1

To

The women in my group and in my life who have helped me find my way to abundance. You are a taste of heaven.

Ken, Katie, and Josh, who I live for. Your love continually rescues me from who I would settle for being.

My kind and gentle King, who pulls me from the mud and takes me flying whenever I have the courage to go.

Contents

Acknowledgments

Several years ago, a friend gave me a wonderful book by Melinda Reinicke called *Parables for Personal Growth*. Melinda's beautifully written stories took me back to my painful places. She helped me remember feelings I'd been protecting myself from while reassuring me that healing was possible. At the end of her parables, she encourages her readers to write a fairy tale of their own. "The Flower Garden," which begins chapter one, is my attempt to tell my own story. I am grateful to Melinda for helping me find a way to tell it.

I am also grateful to . . .

Dr. William and Kristie Gaultiere, who graciously gave me permission to use their material.

Jan Frank, whose teaching over the years has become a part of my thinking process and whose friendship and encouragement on this project have been deeply appreciated.

Sherry Hummel, my counselor, who taught me that feelings would not kill me, who told me the truth so gently, and who held my hand until I believed that my Father could be trusted to hold it.

Dr. Dan Allender, who is not afraid to be associated with me! Thanks for helping me "own the dreams of my heart."

Introduction

Many of us feel stuck in our relationships. We want more closeness and connection, but we don't know how to get them. We are aware in quiet moments that we feel too alone in the world. Friends, family, and God seem to be just beyond reach.

A number of years ago I began meeting with a group of women to find a way out of isolation. As we shared our stories and struggles, we discovered that looking back allowed us to get unstuck and finally move on.

This workbook is designed to help you do the same thing—to find freedom by addressing the old thinking and relating patterns that keep you stuck in your relationships. The personal stories, exercises, and journaling questions are designed to help you explore what holds you back or blocks you from more connectedness.

1 The Flower Garden

A Gift from the King

Many years ago, not far away, a kind and gentle king ruled over a small village. The king loved his people and welcomed them to his castle. The townspeople visited him often to tell him exciting news or ask him for help. Fairies and castle guards helped the king care for the people and carry out his instructions.

One day a beautiful child was born in the village. At the celebration of her birth, fairies from the woodlands came to give the baby a gift from the king— magical seeds harvested from the king's magnificent gardens. Properly cared for, the seeds would produce a garden of beautiful flowers.

The fairies said that every little girl should have a place of loveliness—a place that would reflect her own beauty and remind her of her preciousness to the king. They told the child's parents to guard her garden diligently because the terrible dragon would certainly try to ruin it. Only carefully protected gardens would escape the dragon's destruction.

The dragon hated the fairies and their magical seeds. He despised music and laughter, and the king's flowers inspired both. He was deter-

I have summoned you by name; you are mine. When you pass through the waters, I will be with you; and when you pass through the rivers, they will not sweep over you. When you walk through the fire, you will not be burned; the flames will not set you ablaze.

Isaiah 43:1-2

mined to destroy as many gardens as possible so he could rid the town of its loyalty to the king. Occasionally the dragon would even attack the king's own gardens in an effort to destroy the source of the seeds. But the castle guards never rested and were much stronger. These failures enraged the dragon, increasing his resolve to destroy what he could and avenge his humiliation.

In the beginning, the child's parents were careful, but as time passed without any sign of the dragon, they assured themselves that he must have been defeated by the king's guards.

But the dragon had not been defeated; he knew that people were easily fooled and, given enough time, would become careless.

The little girl's flower garden fell prey to the dragon one night just after she had fallen asleep. She was startled by a loud rushing sound. Then a low growl frightened her so much that she shook from head to toe. From her bed near the window she saw him coming. He flew directly to her garden and began circling, as if savoring the anticipation of destroying it.

She jumped from her bed and raced through the village calling for help, but she could not awaken anyone. She ran back to her window in time to see the dragon send his first blast of fire over her precious flowers. She watched in terror, paralyzed, helpless to protect her garden.

Breathing deeply, the dragon watched the garden burn. Then he noticed her at the window. He laughed when he saw her there silently weeping.

"Ah, little one, I have destroyed your flowers!" he proclaimed triumphantly. "Where are those who say they love you? Could none of them be roused to come to your defense? What a pity!" He laughed again, turned as if to go, but decided he wasn't done with her. He was pleased that the garden was destroyed, but he knew that the fairies would return with their unlimited supply of seeds. His goal was not only to destroy the flowers but also to extinguish the child's longing for beauty. "There's no point in planting again," he sneered. "I will return and ruin whatever I find growing. Your caretakers cannot be trusted to protect you. You will always have to face me alone, and I will always be more powerful than you. Remember, little one, I will come again." Finally, he left.

When he was out of sight, the little girl hurried down to her garden to save what was left of her precious flowers. She ran to the well in the courtyard and began filling water buckets to put out the flames. She spent the remainder of the night carrying bucket after bucket until the smoke cleared. At dawn, the morning sun revealed that not a single flower had survived. Her beautiful garden had become a field of charred flowers and thick mud.

The fairies heard the terrible news and went immediately to the little girl's home to give her more seeds. Reluctantly she took them. She wanted desperately to be surrounded by beautiful, fragrant flowers, but she was terrified of the dragon's return. She determined that she would care for the garden herself because she dared not trust anyone else. She would keep her flowers so wet that they could never again catch fire. But the tiny new seeds were unable to withstand the constant watering and soon died. The fairies continued to bring her new seeds and tried to advise her, but her fear of the dragon compelled her to water incessantly.

Years passed, and the child, now a young woman, despaired of ever being able to grow flowers. She had grown accustomed to living in the mud.

"There is no use hoping for flowers anymore," she convinced herself.

Your eyes are too pure to look on evil; you cannot tolerate wrong. Why then do you tolerate the treacherous? Why are you silent while the wicked swallow up those more righteous than themselves?

Habakkuk 1:13

THE FLOWER GARDEN

"It is best to accept that there will never be a garden. After all, without flowers to anger the dragon, I will not have to worry about his return."

From then on she accepted no new seeds from the fairies. They pleaded with her, but she refused. She had learned to trust no one, not even the king's fairies.

"The mud is not beautiful," she said, "but it is soft and comfortable and requires little tending. Living in the mud is much simpler than continuing to plant and constantly fearing the next attack from the dragon."

The fairies were greatly saddened and told the king. He too was deeply distressed. Immediately he sent a messenger to the young woman with an invitation to visit him at his castle. He wanted to comfort her and tell her that he was going to battle against the dragon on her behalf.

But the young woman turned away the messenger. "I have no need of comfort from the king," she told him.

Each day following, the king sent an attendant to her home with a fresh flower, hoping to awaken her love of beauty and inspire her to plant again. The young woman rejected each of the king's gifts. "Please tell the king to send no more flowers," she finally instructed the messenger. "I no longer yearn for beauty."

One day the young woman was surprised by a visit from the king himself.

"Child," he said, "I have come to take you from the mud. You were never intended to live like this. I have beautiful gardens I want you to see. Take my hand and we will fly to lush places. Will you come with me?"

Suddenly angry, the young woman began to cry. "Why have you come now?" she sobbed. "Where were you when the dragon came? I called for help and no one came. If you are so concerned about me, why did you not come then and save my precious flowers? You cannot be trusted." Then she turned away and asked him to leave.

"Child," he said softly, "you have confused my nature with your experience in the garden. I wept for you when the dragon came. I urged people to help you but no one heeded me. I have always been with you, watching over you. I have wanted so much more for you than this. It is time to leave this place behind. You will never be fully satisfied here. Your soul longs for beauty. Will you hold my hand? Will you let me take you some place higher? I promise I will not drop you. I will not let you fall. It is not in my nature to hurt you."

The young woman turned slowly and looked directly into his face. As she studied his eyes she could see that what he said was true. She reached up and placed her hand in his.

The king smiled and wrapped his hand tightly around hers.

How can I give you up?... How can I hand you over?... For I am God, and not man.

Hosea 11:8-9

"He reached down from on high and took hold of me; he drew me out of deep waters. He rescued me from my powerful enemy, from my foes, who were too strong for me . . . ; he rescued me because he delighted in me" (2 Samuel 22:17-18, 20).

 Journaling

Write about any thoughts or feelings aroused in you as you read this story.

_____

_____

_____

Describe an experience when you lost something precious or felt betrayed or abandoned. When did it occur? Who was involved? What feelings did you have? Write as much as you can about this.

_____

_____

_____

_____

_____

_____

_____

_____

_____

_____

How does it feel right now to think and write about that experience?

_____

_____

_____

_____

_____

_____

_____

_____

_____

_____

_____

_____

_____

_____

_____

_____

_____

_____

_____

_____

Place your name in the blank spaces below and read this verse out loud to yourself.

He reached down from on high and took hold of _____.
*He drew her out of deep waters. He rescued her from her foes who were too
strong for her. He rescued* _____ *because He delighted
in her.*

2 Painful Places

A Cross to Carry

They cried to the
LORD *in their trouble,*
and he saved them from
their distress. He sent forth
his word and healed them; he
rescued them from the
grave.
Psalm 107:19-20

FOR YEARS I felt as if I had just enough of God to make me miserable. Enough to make me desire to please him, to try hard to be good, to serve. Enough to make me aware of the areas where I wasn't measuring up, but not enough to experience peace and freedom. I hoped they would come some day when I became more spiritually mature. So I tried harder. But by the time I was a real grown-up—with a husband, kids, a mortgage, and a minivan—something was still missing. My marriage wasn't working, my friendships were shallow, and I felt ignored by God. I was lonely and tired and angry. So I began to say out loud, "Something is not working here! If God really wants a relationship with me, why can't I feel Him? Why can't I hear Him? If this is as good as it gets, it's not good enough!"

I soon learned that when you get honest, I mean really honest, and you say what you really think and feel—not your Sunday school answer, but the uncensored, ugly truth—people get nervous. Sometimes they will give you a condescending look and suggest a Scripture passage to read or a Bible study to do. Sometimes they will even excuse themselves from a relationship with you. But sometimes they will look very relieved. They will say, "Thank God, I thought I was the only one!" and will join you in the struggle to find out just why life isn't working very well.

God brought women like this into my life—women who were tired of pretending, who had the courage to say what was true for them. And together we have been practicing being real. We have begun to tell our life stories, to acknowledge denied feelings, and to explore the consequences of our experiences. We have been learning to move toward each other in the middle of brokenness, in the middle of sadness and sin. And we have found freedom in speaking the truth; we have seen healing through our sense of community. Somehow this process of honesty and struggle, of looking back as well as forward, has released God's power to bring about growth in our lives.

At a spiritual retreat during my last year of seminary I was working through some directed reading and journaling when I came to Luke 14:27, "Anyone who does not carry his cross and follow me cannot be my disciple." I had always understood this verse as a call to sacrifice, to self-denial, but as I read it that day, I became aware of it in an entirely new way. God used that verse to create an image that would bring about change in my life. Here is my journal entry that day:

February 19

As I think about this verse, a picture is developing in my head. I am standing at one end of a long, twisting hallway. There are many doors on each side of the hallway. Far ahead I can see Jesus. He is going in some doors and out others. I am trying to follow Him but I can't keep up. I look down and see a thick, heavy rope tied to one of my ankles. At the other end of the rope is a large wooden cross lying on the ground. I realize that I have been trying to follow Jesus while dragging this huge cross behind me. Suddenly I am aware that this cross represents my experience of sexual abuse!

I call out for Jesus to wait for me, but He calls back, "Pick up your cross, Elaine. It is the only way you will be able to keep up with me."

"I am fine walking this way," I tell Him.

But He responds, "You must pick it up, look at it, feel it. I will make you strong enough to carry it."

"But Lord, if I pick it up it will become real! It is too ugly! If I pick it up I will be humiliated all over again."

Then the image ended and I wrote this:

All my life I have tried to pretend that my history, this painful place, wasn't important. It was real only when it was happening. When it was over, it was over. It has been over now for years. I have survived it. So it is done. But I am learning that it is still with me. I am still afraid, still angry. I still refuse to trust, to feel, to give and receive love in ways that fulfill me and the people in my life. I see now that "carry-ing my cross" is, in part, about accepting my life story.

God has been taking me on a journey. He has been teaching me that my relationship with Him has not been just about Him and me. It has been clouded by my experiences with flesh-and-blood people. People who were supposed to protect, but didn't. People who were supposed to listen and nurture, but didn't. These experiences and expectations are a part of me, and they affect my ability to trust and to experience love. I cannot shake them off at the door when I enter a new relationship or when I relate to God. These are places in my past where I experienced pain, and they are still with me.

I don't know what the painful places are for you, but I've come to believe that we all have them. For me, it's sexual abuse and the family dynamics that allowed it to happen, but it can also be a hundred other things. Perhaps you were too often ignored, criticized, humiliated, unprotected. Perhaps you lived with expectations that you were never able to meet, feelings and needs that you were not allowed to express. Maybe you were taught that you were lovable only if your behavior and accomplishments met the standards of others. Perhaps your painful place is a childhood filled with adults who abandoned you to pursue alcohol, careers, or romance. Maybe you carry the pain of never knowing the gentle touch of a parent, of never hearing someone say "I love you" with no strings attached. Maybe you have pain related to choices you made looking for love—physical relationships that still haunt you or an abortion you can't talk about.

Ignoring the painful places doesn't make them go away. It keeps us stuck in them—stuck in patterns of self-protection or self-destruction. We hold back in relationships with friends, spouses, and God. Way down deep we are afraid no one, not even God, can really be trusted. We are sure we will be laughed at, used, or left. Being known intimately—emotionally and physically—is too threatening. We must always be on guard—not enough to make anyone notice and call us cold, but just enough to stay safe, to be in control. We use anger, disgust, or ambivalence to push people away.

This workbook will give you an opportunity to explore your own painful places and find out how they're still affecting you. I have included some from my own journey. Some of the women in my group (whose names have been changed) have shared parts of theirs as well. If you find yourself in some of these stories, know that you are not alone.

This material won't take you all the way through the process, but it will get you started. Take your time working through it—perhaps a chapter or so a month—to give yourself time to remember, feel, and write. Write as much as you can about the issues raised. Write about other feelings, thoughts, or experiences that come to mind. Take some friends with you on this journey (a group of four to six women works well) and share your stories, your feelings, your struggles. Meet weekly if possible to talk about what you're learning and experiencing. You will find, no matter what your histories, that you are more alike than different.

I urge you to take a look—a good long look—at the cross you may be dragging behind you. Not just for the sake of looking at it or finding someone to blame for it, but so you can move on to the abundance and freedom that God has waiting for you.

The king is softly whispering, "Child, it's time. I have come to take you from the mud. I know it has been hard for you to live without flowers. Will you come with me?"

Give ear to my words, O LORD, consider my sighing. Listen to my cry for help, my King and my God, for to you I pray.

Psalm 5:1-2

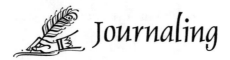 # Journaling

Ask God to make Himself known to you through this process. Ask Him to show you how past relationships have taught you to shut yourself off to present relationships and to all that He longs to give you. Tell Him you want to feel and hear Him. Then listen for His voice.

What might be the cross that you need to pick up and carry? What part of your life story are you afraid to look at?

_____

_____

_____

_____

_____

_____

_____

3 Stuck in the Mud

Trying Harder, Sinking Deeper

I N EVERY woman's heart there lives a little girl. Some little girls have always known how to fly. They have been cherished and nurtured, and for them flying is as natural as breathing. When the king comes, they run to take hold of his hand.

But for many of us, flying is something we only dream of in private, wishful moments. We hear whispers deep within us, "There is a way 'to be' that you have not yet experienced. There is more depth, more meaning, more fulfillment." But we are afraid to believe. We tell ourselves that who we are in our worst moments is all we ever will be. We resign ourselves to living in defeat and berate ourselves for foolishly believing that we could be more. We conclude that flying is for others—those who are stronger, smarter, prettier, thinner. Our painful places have taught us that wanting, dreaming, and hoping lead only to disappointment.

Still, the longings call to us. And there are days when we dare to believe. We picture ourselves as peaceful, healthy, and con-

They were hungry and thirsty, and their lives ebbed away. Then they cried out to the LORD in their trouble, and he delivered them from their distress ... for he satisfies the thirsty and fills the hungry with good things.

Psalm 107:5-6, 9

nected to the people in our lives—free of compulsions, self-protectiveness, and fear. We promise ourselves that the future will be different. Tomorrow will be the start of something new. We will be stronger then. But tomorrow comes accompanied by more failure. And we wonder which is worse—the longing to fly or the struggles that keep us from it.

Life would be so much easier if we could silence the yearnings, if we could give up and come to terms with who and what we are, if we could accept that this is all we ever will be. But the longings will not go away. They are not supposed to.

> Our longings are not a curse. Their pestering persistence is an evidence of supreme possible good. Our longings are meant to keep us searching. If longings exist then that which will fulfill them must exist. That sense propels us— there must be more. The longings demand it. (Jean Fleming, *The Homesick Heart*, NavPress, 21-22.)

What is it that keeps us longing even in the face of anticipated failure? It is the King. The Father has placed His mark on us. We are His creations—image bearers of the great Creator. We are intended for intimacy, created to fly, and the longings are the voice of His Spirit inviting us into His freedom. The sins of others have wounded us, and our own sin has kept us stuck in patterns that resist intimacy. Pain in the past has taught us that attempting to grow leads only to disappointment and embarrassment.

But our painful places need not be the end of our journey. We may be stuck right now, but there is a way to get unstuck.

Getting unstuck requires that we identify the false messages that we believe about ourselves. Messages are the communications we receive from others about who we are. They help define what we believe about how valuable, lovable, and important we are to others. We received these messages in day-to-day experiences with the significant people in our lives (parents, relatives, teachers, pastors, coaches, and friends). Too often, the messages were negative. We heard, "You can't do anything right," "You never use your head," and "You ought to have known better than that." Sighs and scowls reinforced the message that we were an irritation, a disappointment, or a burden.

We lived with people who were careless in their communications. Whether intentionally or not, they taught us to think of ourselves as unacceptable, often addressing our behavior by attacking our person. Instead of telling us our behavior was the problem, they told us that *we* were the problem. Over time, we translated the "You are" messages into "I am" statements, which determined our self-concept and created the lies we live by.

If, for example, you had a parent who often responded to your negative behavior by saying, "You should be ashamed of yourself," you may have internalized that message and embraced it as the truth about yourself. When you make a mistake now, even though you know making mistakes is something everyone does, you believe you should have known better. You berate yourself, telling yourself how ashamed you ought to be for what you've just done. Or perhaps the message was more indirect. Perhaps your family

STUCK IN THE MUD

33

had high expectations about grades, and when you failed to get them your parents responded in a way that said you were less valuable than those who measured up. Over time you learned that the only way to feel loved was through exceptional performance, so even today you feel pressured to perform perfectly.

Rather than help us learn from our mistakes, these messages disable and haunt us, so we search for ways to silence the voices and numb the pain. We discover that such things as shopping, eating, watching television, and being constantly busy keep the bad feelings away, so we use them more and more. Sometimes we withdraw from relationships, withholding emotional or physical intimacy from those who need us because we are afraid of making a mistake or getting hurt again.

The messages are strong. They can undermine our resolve to grow and destroy our hope. We have heard them for so long that we have come to accept them as the truth about ourselves. And the voices are so familiar that they seem like old friends. When someone tries to convince us that the messages are not true, we politely explain that they are mistaken about us.

Over the past few months as I've worked on this material, my own messages have been working overtime. "What do you think you're doing! You don't know what you're talking about. What makes you think you could write anything that would be helpful to anyone! You should know better."

In the beginning, I thought the message was a reality check, but over time I began to recognize the voice from my past. If I close my eyes, I can still see my mother's face—tight, irritated. I can hear the disgust in her voice, "Don't be so stupid. You don't know what you're talking about."

I know she never intended for me to carry those words into adulthood, but the words are still there standing between me and freedom.

 Journaling

By paying attention to your self-talk (what you say to yourself about yourself) you can discover some of your own messages. In the following situations, what might you say to yourself?

When I see someone I admire, I think . . .
(e.g., "I wish I could be important like that, but I'm nothing special.")

_____

_____

When I feel angry at someone, I think . . .
(e.g., "Just let it go. I'm too sensitive. Nobody likes sensitive people.")

_____

_____

When I say something inappropriate to my child or a friend, I think . . .
(e.g., "How could I be such a jerk! I'm always messing things up.")

Kate's Story

One night I was watching a television news program about a custody battle for a ten-year-old girl. She had been adopted at birth, but now, due to a court ruling, was going back to live with her birth mother. The little girl was devastated, being forced to leave the only parents she had ever known. Although the adoptive parents fought very hard to keep her, they lost. I remember thinking how awful she must feel and how abandoned she must feel by her adoptive parents. My emotions were running high. I was really feeling sad for this little girl. Then came the part of the program where you have to guess the date when certain things happened. They flashed three dates on the screen—1979, 1980, 1981. I was thinking, "Please, not 1980." Over and over in my mind I kept saying, "Not 1980, not 1980!" Then two of the dates disappeared, leaving 1980—the year my parents divorced—glaring on the screen. During the commercial break, I sat staring, unable to move, tears spilling from my eyes. The story of the little girl came back on, and as I looked at the girl, I saw myself being abandoned by my mother!

I began to pray, not knowing what all of this meant nor why I was feeling this way now. I felt as if I had hit an all-time low. Why, at thirty years of age, was I grieving the loss of my mother?

I was thirteen when my mom moved out, taking my two older brothers with her and leaving me with my dad, a drug user. Shortly after she left, my father overdosed. I found him slumped in the bathroom. I didn't know what to do. He was sent away to a rehabilitation hospital, and my mom moved back in to take care of me. When he returned, there was a court battle for custody. Although they were granted joint custody, my mother decided to quit fighting with my father and let us live with him. My father remarried when I was fifteen, throwing us into a difficult step-family situation.

I had always blamed my father for all the pain during that time. In my mind the awful divorce that changed my whole life was my father's doing. I believed that if only he hadn't fought so hard, she wouldn't have had to walk away from us. I had never seen that my mother was also responsible. But I realized that night that she had chosen to leave us because it was easier for her. She was free to pursue her own life.

I was angry for days after seeing that television program. Then lights started coming on in other areas of my life. I began to see that much of the way I was living now was attached to the feeling of being abandoned. Small things, like my husband spending an extra hour at the computer rather than with me, or spending the morning playing basketball and not with me. He didn't say it, but I was sure he didn't want to be with me. Why would he? I'm not fun, not special, not lovable, not worth spending time with. I began to realize that those feelings had been there since I was thirteen.

When my mom left, I got the message that I wasn't worth staying for,

I wasn't special enough. I tried begging her, but she left anyway. Her leaving said to me that it didn't matter what I did or how badly I needed her—her new life was more important.

Whenever my husband wanted to be away from me, the same feelings surfaced. My fear of being alone again kept me circling around him, trying to make sure he would never abandon me. I couldn't stop my mom from leaving, but I had a second chance in my marriage. I was determined to do whatever it took to keep him from leaving—even if it meant nagging. But even when he stayed the message wouldn't go away, "You're not worth it. He's only here because you made him stay." If I was worthy of his attention, he'd want to be with me every minute; I wouldn't have to force him. It was a no-win situation. No matter how much time he spent with me, it was never enough to put my fear to rest. My behavior was confusing and suffocating to him. But I thought it was normal to want to be with him every minute. I thought he deserved my anger for wanting to be with others. If he really loved me I was sure he'd want to be with me as much as I wanted to be with him.

> See, I am doing a new thing! Now it springs up; do you not perceive it? I am making a way in the desert and streams in the wasteland.
>
> Isaiah 43:19

God started slowly whispering to me, showing me how much of the way I was operating in my marriage was attached to that feeling of abandonment. I was trying to avoid that feeling by demanding that my husband make me feel secure. Slowly, I began to deal with the truth. I began sifting through the facts, facing the damage of those years and the messages I had been living with since then.

Below are messages that you may recognize. Check any statements that sound familiar. Does a voice, a face, or an incident come to mind? If so, write the name or the situation beside the statement.

_____ You must be good to be loved.
_____ It's not okay to make mistakes.
_____ We will reject you if you make a mistake.
_____ If you mess up too badly, God will not be able to use you.
_____ Your value is based on what others think of you.
_____ If you don't do for others, you are not valuable.
_____ You are weak, only weak people cry.
_____ We love you if things are going well.
_____ Being good is more important than anything.
_____ Just ignore things that upset you. Don't rock the boat.
_____ You shouldn't be struggling with anger, food, depression, etc., you are a Christian.
_____ Don't be so stupid.
_____ Don't be so selfish.
_____ You should be ashamed of yourself.
_____ You don't care about anyone but yourself.
_____ You don't know what you're talking about.
_____ I wish you'd never been born.
_____ You're a trouble-maker.
_____ You're a disappointment.

_____ You are too sensitive/too emotional.
_____ You never get anything right.
_____ What were you thinking?
_____ Why don't you ever use your head?
_____ You are a bad girl/boy.
_____ Other

_____

_____

_____

Think about the last time you were in the following situations. Describe what happened, who was involved, and how you responded. What feelings did you experience? Try to think beyond your initial responses. What other emotions may have been there?

You made a mistake or failed at something.

_____

_____

_____

_____

A friend disappointed or hurt you.

_____

_____

_____

You were anxious about something.

_____

_____

_____

What kind of messages came up in those situations? Refer to previous pages for help with possible messages.

_____

_____

_____

Identify one of the strongest messages you received during childhood. Write about an event or situation when you received the message.

A message I got in childhood was . . .

_____

I received this message when . . .

_____

_____

_____

_____

It may be affecting my behavior in this way . . .

_____

_____

_____

What messages might you be passing on to your family or friends? (Think about the things you say to your spouse or children when you are upset.)

_____

_____

_____

_____

_____

How do these messages limit or damage relationships with people you want to be closer to?

_____

_____

_____

_____

What could you do the next time you realize you're hearing an old message? (e.g., journal, talk with a friend, express what you're feeling to God.)

_____

4 Finding the Spot that Hurts

It's Time to Stop Settling for Numbness

AS CHILDREN many of us coped with pain by shutting down our true feelings and turning off who we really were. We learned early that no one was really interested in what we felt and that expressing ourselves would lead only to disappointment or rejection. So we adapted. And we discovered that making ourselves "disappear" or finding an important role to fill helped us numb the pain.

> O LORD, do not forsake me; be not far from me, O my God. Come quickly to help me, O Lord my Savior.
>
> Psalm 38:21-22

[W]e either flee our own reality or manufacture a false self which is mostly admirable, mildly prepossessing, and superficially happy. We hide what we know or feel ourselves to be (which we assume to be unacceptable and unlovable) behind some kind of appearance which we hope will be more pleasing. We hide behind pretty faces which we put on for the benefit of our public. And in time we may even come to forget that we are hiding, and think that our assumed pretty face is what we really look

like. (Simon Tugwell, "The Beatitudes," Soundings in Christian Tradition, Springfield, IL: Templegate Publishers, 1980, 130, quoted in Brennan Manning, *Abba's Child*, NavPress, 1944, 18).

In *Abba's Child* author Brennan Manning writes about his own journey to painful places. He tells about the twenty days he spent isolated in a cabin, meeting with a psychologist in the morning and spending the rest of the day in solitude and silence.

As the days passed, I realized that I had not been able to feel anything since I was eight years old. A traumatic experience at that time shut down my memory for the next nine years and my feelings for the next five decades. When I was eight, the impostor, or false self, was born as a defense against pain. The impostor within whispered, "Brennan, don't ever be your real self anymore because nobody likes you as you are. Invent a new self that everybody will admire and nobody will know." So I became a good boy—polite, well-mannered, unobtrusive, and deferential. I studied hard, scored excellent grades, won a scholarship in high school, and was stalked every waking moment by the terror of abandonment and the sense that nobody was there for me. I learned that perfect performance brought the recognition and approval I desperately sought. I orbited into an unfeeling zone to keep fear and shame at a safe distance. As my therapist remarked, "All these years there has been a steel trapdoor covering your emotions and denying you access to them." Meanwhile,

the impostor I presented for public inspection was non-chalant and carefree. The great divorce between my head and my heart endured throughout my ministry. For eighteen years I proclaimed the good news of God's passionate, unconditional love—utterly convicted in my head but not feeling it in my heart. (Manning, *Abba's Child*, 21-22).

Getting unstuck requires speaking the truth about our history, allowing ourselves to feel the pain we've so long denied or avoided, and connecting those experiences to our patterns of relating today.

Jill's Story

May 1995

I am tired of working so hard to gain people's approval, of trying to live up to this ideal that I think God wants. I am tired of believing I can never be quite good enough. My doubts and distrust in myself are getting in my way. I don't know why the approval of other people is so important to me. I read stories that show God's power, but they seem too far removed from me. Why do others have such strong faith and get so excited about reading the Bible and I don't? I don't really feel the power and presence of God. What am I doing wrong?

Please, God, show Yourself and Your power to me. Help me see what I'm missing.

June 1995

In high school, when I first accepted Jesus, I thought that would take care of all my problems—surely my dad would stop drinking if I prayed hard enough and did all the "right" things. I thought that all the effects of my chaotic family would just disappear with that little prayer. I think going my own way in college was about feeling like You weren't doing what You were supposed to do. You didn't make me feel better by taking away my pain and anger. Today, in group, I realized that I still have to deal with the pain and anger that come from my childhood. I need to see how my feelings, thoughts, and behaviors now are influenced by all those years.

September 1995

I'm trying to process all the stuff we talked about today, trying to figure out what I'm feeling. Most of the time I don't show what I'm feeling. I get irritated with people often, but I don't know what's behind the irritation. I feel like crying right now. I feel that lump in my throat, the pounding of my heartbeat. I feel like I could throw up! I'm full of nervousness, anticipation. What's going on? Why am I feeling this way? God, I'm trying to be still and listen—should I read? What? Tell me what!...

While Jill waited and listened, she became aware of her feelings about her dad.

I feel so sad. I hate my dad. I really think I do. I'm not supposed to, but I do. I didn't want him around. I wanted him to die and then he did. What do I do with that? What does that mean about me?

I'm supposed to respect my parents. I have no respect for him. How could I when life was the way it was? Never knowing what to expect. Waking up at 6 A.M. to find him already drunk, wondering if he'd be there to pick me up from school. If he was there, would he be drunk or mad? If he didn't show, there was the anxiety about what I would find when I got home. Sometimes it was a relief to get there and find him passed out on the couch, on the bed, or on the porch if he didn't make it inside. At least then he would be out for a while. There was no way to know what would happen when he woke up. He could be angry and screaming or he could leave to find more alcohol. If he left, there was the worry about whether he'd make it back or not. Would he kill himself or someone else? Would he get arrested and give us one night of peace? There was the screaming and yelling, breaking things, throwing furniture through the windows, verbal attacks. He never showed up to my high school graduation. He made it to my wedding—drunk. When I look at those pictures now, I almost wish he hadn't been there.

So much hurt and embarrassment.

As a child I felt responsible for doing everything just right so that he wouldn't get mad. But there was no way to know what was "right" because it would change from day to day, hour to hour, minute to minute. Hoping at least to please my mom so she wouldn't be so stressed out when she got home, I would clean up, get dinner going,

FINDING THE
SPOT THAT HURTS

stay out of trouble. Keep up the image of looking good on the outside. I'm still doing that today, even though he is dead.

November 1995

I realized today that I'm still taking responsibility for my childhood family. I still feel like their happiness or destruction is based on me. I have always been the one to take care of things and make sure everyone is okay. If they're not, it's my fault. I didn't do or say the right thing. I have to be in control of all situations so that things go the right way and everyone stays okay. I know this is ridiculous thinking! But I feel anxious when I don't fix situations or protect others. I'm supposed to rescue everyone. If I don't, something bad will happen and it will be my fault. I'm supposed to always be good, otherwise people will feel permission to make bad choices because of me. It's an overwhelming responsibility and more than anyone can do. I don't really have that kind of power, but I automatically feel responsible when others are in trouble. I want to feel that I am worthy of being loved without doing all these things. I'm sure that this is reflected in my image of You, God. I constantly feel as if I must perform to earn Your acceptance.

Jill's painful place was a childhood devastated by alcoholism. Rather than face the pain of his own past, her father abandoned his children to numb himself. He was violent and abusive. Jill's mom failed to protect her children from his rage and the chaos that became their family system. Jill learned that she would have to take care of herself and, in order to be of any significance in the family, to take care of everyone else as well. She invented a new self. She became a mother to her younger siblings, trying to fix the damage her dad did, trying to find ways to take away the pain for them. She put huge expectations on herself. She must always rescue, always fix things, always smooth things over, always be good.

 Journaling

Think about a time when the responses of others taught you that it wasn't okay to be honest about what you needed or wanted. Write about it. What did that situation teach you?

_____

_____

_____

_____

_____

_____

_____

_____

_____

Complete the following statements.

"Don't be your real self because . . ."

_____

_____

_____

_____

_____

_____

_____

_____

_____

_____

"Invent a new self that is . . ."

_____

_____

_____

_____

_____

_____

_____

_____

For Jill, getting unstuck meant allowing herself to feel feelings she had not acknowledged—feelings she thought were wrong or selfish. It meant admitting that her parents had failed her in very important ways and that she was still living with the consequences of those failures. She also had to admit that she had felt terrified, confused, and ignored as a child, that she was angry at her dad and disappointed in her mom. She began to work on changing her role in the family and letting them take responsibility for their own problems so that she could more fully concentrate on her own family and friendships.

Walking through this process helped her become more comfortable with her real self. She learned that there were relationships in which it was acceptable to feel and express anger or hurt, where she could make mistakes and not be responsible for taking care of everyone all the time.

Allowing yourself to see and feel the truth is the first step to freedom and flying. Those of us who are more comfortable living in our heads have a hard time seeing the point of resurrecting all this painful stuff. But, as John Powell reminds us in *Why Am I Afraid to Love?* . . .

When you repress or suppress those things which you don't want to live with, you don't really solve the problem because you don't bury the problem dead—you bury it alive. It remains alive and active inside of you.

Staying stuck is easier. But it means that you will continually deny yourself and others of knowing the real you. You will not have access to a full range of feelings—good and bad. You will have to choose between self-protection and connection.

 ## Journaling

The following list will help you identify some of the patterns of thinking that keep you disconnected from others. Check the statements that apply to you.

_____ I believe feelings are a weakness to be ignored or controlled.

_____ I am more comfortable ignoring or controlling feelings.

_____ I feel anxious when others express emotion.

_____ I am uncomfortable needing others.

_____ I am afraid to be vulnerable, to be really known by another person.

_____ Others tell me that they can't get close to me.

_____ I often feel angry, anxious, or depressed.

_____ I tend to hold things in and then overreact.

_____ There are painful experiences in my past that I have never talked to anyone about (or that I am unwilling or unable to talk about).

_____ I feel very distant from God.

_____ I feel that God is usually angry with me or disappointed in me.

_____ When I feel upset I use things like shopping, eating, watching television, or cleaning to help me feel better.
_____ I have a hard time sitting still; I am usually very busy.
_____ My relationships lack intimacy.

Pick three or four of the above statements that you strongly relate to and write about them.

_____

_____

_____

_____

_____

_____

_____

_____

Listed below are characteristics that describe the best and worst of families. Think about your family of origin and evaluate how it worked in regard to each characteristic. Mark an X on the continuum at the place which best represents your family. Take your time and allow yourself to remember life as a child. In the margins, write about any experiences or interactions that come to mind as you think through each characteristic.

Nurturing	Non-Nurturing

Accepting, respectful environment | Judging, critical, tense environment

1 ——————————————————————————— 10

Rules are consistent but can also be flexible | Rules are unclear, non-existent, or rigid

1 ——————————————————————————— 10

Differences are accepted, celebrated | Differences are discouraged, rejected; conformity is expected

1 ——————————————————————————— 10

Growth and achievements are encouraged | Achievements are required, ignored, minimized

1 ——————————————————————————— 10

Communication is regular, open, clear | Communication is infrequent; conflict is constant

1 ——————————————————————————— 10

Consequences for negative behavior are appropriate and consistent | Consequences for negative behavior are inconsistent, shaming

1 ——————————————————————————— 10

Members are comfortable talking about feelings | Members carefully guard their own feelings

1 ——————————————————————————— 10

A wide range of feelings and topics are expressed and discussed	Only certain feelings and topics are tolerated

1 ——————————————————————— 10

Few shoulds	Lots of shoulds, controlling

1 ——————————————————————— 10

Members are valued for themselves regardless of their performance	Members are valued for performance or roles they fulfill in the family

1 ——————————————————————— 10

Now write about your family. What feelings were acceptable to express in your family? Which were unacceptable? How did you know the difference?

_____

_____

_____

_____

_____

_____

_____

What made people angry in your family?

_____

_____

_____

_____

What were the consequences for making a mistake or breaking a family rule?

_____

_____

_____

_____

_____

What were some "shoulds" in your family?

_____

I sought the LORD,
and he answered me; he
delivered me from all my
fears. Those who look to him are
radiant; their faces are never
covered with shame.

Psalm 34:4-5

_____

_____

_____

_____

_____

_____

_____

_____

_____

_____

Pay attention to how you feel right now. How did you feel about filling out the continuum and writing about your family? Was it a relief or did you feel as if you were betraying them? Were you anxious? Numb?

_____

_____

_____

_____

_____

_____

_____

_____

_____

_____

_____

_____

_____

_____

_____

_____

This is an important step. Allow yourself to sit with the feelings that have come up and acknowledge them. Talk to someone you trust about what you've written. Do something nurturing for yourself—

go for a walk or run,
cuddle with your kids,
go get a "foo-foo" coffee.

5 Wounds and Bondage

Finding the Courage to Feel

PEOPLE OFTEN ask me, "What is the point of bringing up all these feelings and memories from the past? Why is it necessary to talk about things that happened so long ago? What do they have to do with who I am today?"

When our painful places are never acknowledged, and when the "mud" they created in our thinking patterns is not recognized, we may feel very "stuck" in adulthood. Many of us know this "stuck" feeling. We have felt so trapped in behavior and relating patterns that change seems impossible. We want things to be better but trying harder doesn't work. We are unable to understand or express our deepest feelings, unable to create fulfilling intimacy in our relationships. The point of addressing the past is to get freedom from it. When we allow ourselves to feel denied feelings, to tell untold stories, and to make connections between our histories and our present patterns, we will finally get "unstuck."

Several years ago, our group helped organize a weekend

Save me, O God, for the waters have come up to my neck. I sink in the miry depths, where there is no foothold. I have come into the deep waters; the floods engulf me. I am worn out calling for help; my throat is parched. My eyes fail, looking for my God.

Psalm 69:1-3

WOUNDS AND BONDAGE

retreat for women who wanted to look at these issues with us. Jan Frank, a therapist and author, was our speaker. She talked about the concept of wounds and bondages to help us see how painful places keep us stuck. She held up a doll, wrapped in bandages from head to toe, and said that many of us were like the doll. Underneath the bandages, she explained, the doll was covered with cuts, bruises, and open sores. These wounds represented broken trusts, disappointments, rejections, or abandonments. As children, we had no way to heal these wounds, so we found ways to make them less painful. We learned to cope by shutting down our feelings or distracting ourselves with activities. But the wounds were still there, *are* still there, though much of the time we are not even aware of them. We think of those experiences as something we left behind long ago. But there is a pain we can't identify. We often feel depressed, angry, or anxious. When we don't understand why, we revert to our old ways of coping.

The bandages represent our attempts to cover the pain. We use all kinds of things to cover emotional wounds—food, alcohol, TV, perfectionism, achievements, relationships, shopping, sex, work, busyness. We need something to take the edge off the pain. Over time these bandages become our bondage. At first we controlled them, using them only to help us feel better. But now they control us, making us feel ashamed of how often we use them. We hide our behavior from others. We understand that we are damaging our bodies and our relationships but we feel powerless to change.

Rather than address the wound that is causing the pain, we focus all our energy on the bondage. The consequences of our bondage is more identifiable: using food causes us to gain weight, over-spending puts us in financial trouble, sexual addictions destroy our marriages. We think the bondage is the problem. "If I could just stop _____, everything would be okay." We work hard trying to get these behaviors under control, only to find that success doesn't last for long. We try harder. We find ourselves involved again. Feeling defeated. Living in secret.

I started binge eating at age fifteen. I don't remember making a choice to use food to make myself feel better. I had no idea why I wanted to eat so much more than my body needed; I just knew it comforted me. By the time I was in college, I was eating every day until I was sick, then taking large amounts of laxatives to purge. I woke up sick every morning and went to bed sick every night. I couldn't purge fast enough to keep up. I began to put on weight. I felt too ugly and ashamed to tell anyone. I kept my bizarre eating habits a secret from everyone. I hated myself, but I felt powerless to stop. I begged God to change me, but He seemed content to remain silent. Food had become my bondage, and I could not release myself from it.

When I graduated from college, I went into full-time youth ministry and over time was able to use food less and less. Ministry became my distraction. It helped me feel important. I loved the kids and they loved me. I had found a better way to dull the ache. By the time I married in my late twenties, I was eating normally, happy with my body, and feeling free from compulsive eating. I thought it was over. But I had never dealt with the wounds.

Ken and I had been married about eight years when we came to a crisis point. I felt completely hopeless, unsure about whether it was even possible to repair what was wrong with our relationship. We decided to try counseling. I went hoping Sherry, our counselor, could fix what was wrong with Ken. I had tried fixing him for eight years but it had only pushed him away from me. I thought maybe an objective professional would have more effect!

She asked about my history in one of our first sessions, and I gave her the facts of my life—sexual abuse included. I could talk about it easily because I had no feelings about it. She stopped me and asked if I had ever addressed the abuse. I proudly reported that I had read a book about it a number of years ago, told my family so they could protect my nieces and nephews, and asked God to help me forgive my uncle. So yes, I had addressed it. She said that perhaps it would be a good idea if she and I met alone and did a little more work. This was not what I had in mind!

As she and I talked about those events over the next few months, I began to feel feelings I had refused to acknowledge since I was a child—shame, embarrassment, terror, and anger all came flooding back. I wanted to run away again. Looking at the wound was painful—so painful I started using food again.

Here are some of my journal entries written during the time my bondage resurfaced.

March 1996

I say over and over that I wish I could let go of using food. That I know it doesn't fill the hole inside. That I will try again. Tomorrow I will use more self-control. But that is not the truth. The truth is I don't hate my struggle with food. I want to binge, want to hurt myself. There is something so comforting about letting go, giving in to the food. Giving up trying to be more than I am. Numbing out. Freeing myself from the work of becoming stronger.

The truth is, I am afraid to let go of food. I am afraid to fly, afraid to go where You want to take me, afraid to be peaceful. Life has always been hard, lonely. Isn't that how it's supposed to be? I am so used to sitting here in the mud where it is warm and comfortable. Lord, help me to want healing and deliverance from what holds me to the ground.

April 1996

I listen to a girlfriend talk about letting go of food, about the progress she is making, the freedom that is coming. I smile and tell her I'm happy for her. But inside I'm in a panic, I want to scream, "Who will be there for you if you let go of food?" I think of this compulsion as a friend! Someone who holds me in my worst moments. I don't know how to live without it. I don't want to live without it.

May 1996

I feel so alone against this enemy—the compulsion to destroy myself. It comes so quickly that it arrives before I even feel it approach. I do not wish to overcome it. I allow myself to be paralyzed, allow it to sweep over me, like a huge dark shadow. By then it is too big, too powerful for me to fight against. Honestly, there is no fight in me. I have learned my victim lesson well. I lie still until it is over. Not because it is in reality stronger than I and my Healer but because I believe in it. I believe its voice that I am nothing, will be nothing, will always be too much of a coward to fight back, to free myself and fly. I am not afraid of being miserable, I am not afraid of wasting my life. I am afraid of not being miserable. I am afraid of flying.

Turn your ear

to me, come quickly to

my rescue; be my rock of

refuge, a strong fortress to

save me. . . . Free me from

the trap that is set for me,

for you are my refuge.

Psalm 31:2, 4

God and I are in a tug of war. He says, "Let go of the food so we can fly." He holds me and pulls gently saying, "Come, Elaine, I want to take you flying. Will you let go? Will you let me take you someplace higher? There are beautiful places you have never seen. I promise I will not drop you, I will not let you fall. It is not in my nature to hurt you."

───✦───

Many of us have behaviors in our lives that control us. We feel ashamed and weak, powerless to change, to let go of these behaviors. When we are actively involved in them, we are sure there is no way out. Sometimes we don't want a way. So where do we start?

We start by walking in the light. First John 1:5-10 talks about walking in the light and the role of fellowship and confession in dealing with sin. Gene McConnell, who speaks on the issue of sexual addiction, says that we often remain in bondage because we don't understand what repentance is. He says repentance is not just feeling bad about what we've done (that's remorse) or making up for our sin (penance). Rather, it's restoration—the willingness to enter a process of moving from sin to healing. He believes that "walking in the light" (i.e., in honesty with ourselves and others about our condition) is essential to restoration. "Walking in darkness" is walking in hiddenness and secrecy—pretending we're doing okay, that we can handle things on our own. But "walking in the light" means we position ourselves to live in openness.

Repentance doesn't mean we promise never to fall again (we all know how well that works!). It means we choose to live in honesty. We start by telling the truth to ourselves and to others who can be trusted. As we do, we will find that their acceptance will make all the difference. Their belief that there is good in us, that we can move beyond our destructive patterns, provides strength that we cannot find in isolation.

Experiencing grace from others helps us believe that God could really be on our side, that He could really desire to embrace us just as we are. Then we will understand that the next failure doesn't have to define who we are, that freedom will take time and practice, but it will come.

[I]f we walk in the light, as he is in the light, we have fellowship with one another, and the blood of Jesus, his Son, purifies us from all sin.

1 John 1:7

Therefore confess your sins to each other and pray for each other so that you may be healed. The prayer of a righteous man is powerful and effective.

James 5:16

 # Journaling

Telling the truth about our bondage and discovering how it's connected to our wounds loosens its grip on us. What bondage keeps you from living fully connected to the people in your life? To God?

_____

_____

_____

_____

_____

Write about how it feels to live with this bondage. What are your feelings about it—shame, anger, frustration, hopelessness?

_____

_____

_____

_____

_____

_____

_____

_____

_____

_____

Recall your earliest memory of this behavior. When and why did you involve yourself in this behavior? Write about your history with this bondage.

_____

_____

_____

It's easy to focus our attention and energy on the bondage by trying to control or erase it. However, this behavior is not our biggest problem. Even though the bondage can create no end of trouble in our lives, it is important to understand that it is a response to underlying pain and is only a symptom of the problem. Unless we uncover the wounds, we are unlikely to gain long-term freedom from our bondage. We are more likely to let go of one bondage only to find ourselves trapped in another.

Tess's Story

I was four years old when one of my older brothers began molesting me. It became a way of life for me for the next ten years. No one ever knew. That made it pretty easy to disconnect from it. Yet I felt so different from other little girls. There was an innocence and a carefreeness that I lacked. I chose misfits and outsiders to be my friends. There was a comfort in being around others who didn't fit the mold.

When I became a Christian in fifth grade, I began to feel this overwhelming ache inside. It was like waking up to what was happening. I couldn't pretend anymore. But it had become such a pattern in my life that I didn't know how to make it stop. I began to feel bad about who I was and I had this huge sense of shame. So I tried to make it stop, but he refused to leave me alone. My feelings didn't matter. He didn't even see my pain. He never did. He just needed a warm body to feed his perversion. The ritual would always start the same. He would approach me; I would say no; he would continue; I would beg him to stop; he would tell me I wanted it, that I knew it felt good; I would get confused because the physical sensations were there, so it felt good and yet it felt awful all at the same time. I would try to disappear, to run away mentally, but I couldn't anymore. I just felt bad, dirty, and very alone.

One night when I was fourteen and feeling horrible about myself, I made a decision during a Wednesday night Bible study that "it" was never going to happen again. So the next time he approached me, I told him no. He continued. I was pushing him off, telling him to stop, but he wouldn't. I felt like a caged animal, and panic swept over me. I went crazy. I began biting, pulling hair, doing anything I could to make him stop. That was the last time it ever happened. From then on, he ignored me. He was cold and distant. I thought I was special to him. It was painful to realize that his so-called love for me depended on me behaving the way he wanted me to.

My sexuality lay dormant for a few years. I was repulsed by any type of sexual activity. When I was seventeen, I began dating a young man who I was convinced loved me. After eight months of dating, he let me know he was interested in more than just a kiss. I was overcome with fear and sorrow. I wanted our relationship to remain pure. He promised he would never hurt me. He broke his promise. He turned out to be just as manipulative as my brother. I was devastated at the loss of my virginity. I tried to stop having sex but for many reasons I felt powerless to change. I felt guilty all the time. Trying to be a good Christian wasn't working so I decided to abandon my relationship with God. It was too painful to feel like a failure all the time.

By the time I was nineteen, I had learned how to use my sexuality to get power. I had always been powerless but now I was in control. Having sex was not about sex, it was about controlling the other person. Now I decided when it would start and when it would stop.

Then I met John, a strong man with integrity and morals. He possessed the strength I lacked. He made me feel safe and loved. I completely relied on him to keep me good, to keep me moral. My need to have power and control disappeared. We were married two years later. I recreated myself and made myself into what I believed was the perfect wife. For the first four years of our marriage, we were very happy but then it stopped working. John withdrew from me more and more until it felt like he had disappeared. I thought if I was a good wife, I could make him love me. Nothing I did worked. I felt abandoned and frustrated. I could no longer draw upon his strength. I was alone again. Eventually, my pain turned to anger and I began to act out. I once again sought out friends who were different from the norm. The majority of them were homosexuals who were struggling for an identity, struggling to fit in, struggling to make their pain stop. I experienced a strange comfort in their presence. The badness I felt inside didn't seem so dark when I was with them. The darkness comforted me, and the light brought too much pain, so I let the darkness take over. For me that meant developing my identity around my sexuality. I flirted at work and dressed provocatively. There was a great sense of power when I could make other men want me. This behavior led me down a path of destruction. I became involved with someone at work and separated from my husband. I went back to him after several months for the sake of my son, but I was miserable.

I knew that I lacked the strength to make my marriage work, so out of desperation, I reached out to God. Our family started going to church, and I joined a women's group there. I began to share my life with these women. I realized that I wasn't so bad, that my life wasn't much different from theirs. We all had painful places and we all had developed coping mechanisms to deal with them. Getting free from my bondage meant I had to deal with the abuse and understand the things it had taught me to believe about myself. When I look back on it now, I realize that the way I was wounded taught me to get my self-worth from being wanted, from being sexual. It taught me that when your reality is painful, you create a new one. When my marriage became painful, I recreated a new reality. The affair was a way to escape my life. It wasn't so much that I wanted out of my marriage, I just wanted the pain to stop. Being sexual also helped confirm my belief about myself—that I was bad. Getting free from the bondage required changing my identity to a new identity in Christ. Letting go of my old identity took a long time. I had to change the way I dressed, the way I talked, walked, my whole attitude.

I found that underneath everything was my belief that I couldn't trust God. I wanted the control and the power. Giving God the control and power meant anything could happen to me and I wasn't sure I could handle that. But God was gentle and good. He used wonderful women who affirmed me and encouraged the good in me. These deep connections helped me understand the love and compassion that God has for me. I slowly removed the bandages that I had used to protect my wounds and started the process of healing. God has been faithfully healing me and restoring my marriage and my relationship with Him.

 # Journaling

What wounds does your bondage cover? Write about possible connections between your painful places and your bondage.

_____

_____

_____

_____

_____

_____

_____

_____

"But I will

restore you to health

and heal your wounds,"

declares the LORD . . .

Jeremiah 30:17

See! The winter is past; the

rains are over and gone.

Flowers appear on the

earth; the season of

singing has come . . .

Song 2:11-12

What might happen in your relationships, in your life, if you let go of this bondage? What might you feel more of?

_____

_____

_____

_____

_____

_____

_____

_____

_____

Read the following excerpt from *Abba's Child*.

> What does it mean to feel you are in a safe place? . . . I
> wrote in my journal: To feel safe is to stop living in my
> head and sink down into my heart and feel liked and
> accepted. . . . not having to hide anymore and distract
> myself with books, television, movies, ice cream, shallow
> conversation . . . staying in the present moment and not
> escaping into the past or projecting into the future, alert
> and attentive to the now . . . feeling relaxed and not nerv-
> ous or jittery . . . no need to impress or dazzle others or
> draw attention to myself . . . Unself-conscious, a new way
> of being with myself, a new way of being in the world . . .
> calm, unafraid, no anxiety about what's going to happen
> next. Loved and valued . . . just being together as an end
> in itself. (Manning, 23)

What would it mean to you to feel as if you were in a safe place?
Describe what it would be like.

God sets the
lonely in families, he
leads forth the prisoners
with singing . . .

Psalm 68:6

Is there a person or a group of people with whom you could begin to share your story of bondage? Write about how you might make that happen. What might you say?

Write your name in the blank and read this verse out loud.

The eternal God is _____'s refuge, and underneath her are the everlasting arms. He will thrust out the enemy from before her and will say, "Destroy" (from Deuteronomy 33:27).

6 When God Gets Hooked to the Pain

Making Connections

MOST OF us rarely discuss our feelings about God. We talk about our thoughts and beliefs. We talk about truth and our identity in Christ, but somehow little of this translates into real experience. We believe intellectually that God is kind and forgiving, merciful and interested in our lives, yet we often feel distant from Him, guilty, judged. We are afraid that we are a disappointment to Him, that we don't measure up, and that our needs are of little interest to Him.

For many of us the gap between our thoughts (what we believe about God based on our knowledge of the Bible) and our feelings (how we feel about God based on our experiences with Him) is like a huge chasm. Somehow it's possible to believe all the right things about God, to desire a deep relationship with Him, and yet feel very alone in His presence.

"For I know the plans I have for you," declares the LORD, "plans to prosper you and not to harm you, plans to give you hope and a future."

Jeremiah 29:11

Here is what I wrote about my own struggle in trying to reconcile my knowledge with my feelings:

August 1995

God, far underneath all my theology are secret fears that pull me away from you. I keep my guard up as if I need to protect myself from you, as if you are a dirty trick player, a manipulator. I am afraid that the good things you are doing in my life these days are intended to woo me, to make me believe you care about me. And when I do, you will pull the rug out from under me. I am so afraid you will betray me if I drop my guard.

I remember what betrayal feels like . . .

I am a little girl. My uncle tells me I am pretty, that I am special. He wants to take pictures of me because I am so pretty. I believe him because I want so badly to be special to someone.

It is nighttime. He is outside my door again. Always outside my door. I am terrified, trapped. I pull the pillows and blankets in around me, tuck them in tight, hoping they will protect me. But nothing and no one will protect me from him. He woos me, then he betrays me. I am only here for his amusement.

Today I am a grown woman and I am still holding my breath, waiting for the next betrayal. I read Jeremiah 29:11: "I know the plans I have for you," declares the LORD, "Plans to prosper you and not to harm you, plans to give you hope and a future." Lord, I want so badly to

believe that this is true, that this is who you really are, but I cannot let go of this fear that good things always have strings attached, that you give good things as a way of setting me up, of making me drop my guard so you can betray me. If I abandon myself to you, will you destroy me? Am I only here for your amusement?

We know that we need God's intervention to gain freedom from bondage, but we secretly wonder if God really wants to rescue us. We know we are supposed to run to Him, to "Let go and let God," but sometimes we feel as if all of our pounding on the doors of heaven is pointless.

Why is this? What creates this distance?

Part of the answer lies in the way we've learned to relate to God. We've been taught to focus on right beliefs and right behaviors. We've gotten stuck trying to please God in the same way we try to please the people in our lives. We've never learned how to feel God or how to hear His voice. We talk about joy, peace, and abundance but we have no idea what they really "look" like. Our longings tell us that we need more from Him, but we feel selfish for asking and helpless to pursue it. If God really wants us to be close to Him, why does He seem to make Himself impossible to get close to? If God is truly available for the kind of intimacy David talks about in the Psalms, why can't we experience Him

The LORD is close to the broken-hearted and saves those who are crushed in spirit.

Psalm 34:18

The LORD is near to all who call on him, to all who call on him in truth.

Psalm 145:18

that way? We are reading, praying and serving, but something is wrong.

As the members of our group struggled with these questions, each of us discovered barriers within us that kept God at arm's length. We couldn't see or hear Him clearly because our past experiences stood in the way. We were stuck in ways of relating to God that we had been taught, expecting from Him what we had learned from others to expect.

It wasn't until we began to understand how our past relationships were still affecting our present relationships—not only with others but also with God—that we were able to begin experiencing Him in a deeper way.

All we have to do is look at our behaviors and relationships to find evidence that fears are there. When we fear that we are unacceptable, we strive to perform bigger and better. When we fear that we've not been forgiven, we live with shame, hiding our true selves or trying to make up for the past. When we fear that God is not really involved in our circumstances, we worry and work and strategize as if we are all alone, responding to Him as if He, too, will ultimately fail to accept, rescue, or protect us.

Need more evidence? Look at what happened in your life this past week.

O God,

you are my God,

earnestly I seek you;

my soul thirsts for

you, my body longs for

you, in a dry and

weary land where

there is no water.

Psalm 63:1

- When did your stress level get so high that you or someone else had to pay for it because you were unable to rest in God's arms?

- Whom did you try to control out of fear that you couldn't rely on God to work in the situation?

- What did you use to comfort or numb yourself because you didn't feel nurtured by Him when you were lonely or frustrated?

If we really believed, I mean, *really* believed, that God could be trusted in every circumstance, wouldn't our lives look different?

Let's find out what is standing in the way.

 # Journaling

The following questionnaire will help you identify the specific aspects of God's character that you have trouble experiencing or feeling. We will be looking at fourteen attributes of God. This is not an exhaustive list, but it is a place to start. This questionnaire measures your *feelings* about God, not your knowledge or intellectual beliefs, so be sure to answer the questions based on how you "sometimes feel." Try to be completely honest. It is often difficult for people to answer these questions because they are uncomfortable saying, for example, that sometimes they feel as if God is not paying much attention to them. It doesn't "feel right" because they know it is not the truth about God. Unfortunately, it may very accurately represent unrecognized fears or anxieties they are experiencing in their relationship with Him.

Each statement is designed to help you determine your feelings about God, so don't respond in terms of what you believe, think, or "know" about Him. Instead, read each statement in light of your feelings and experiences. Then circle either "T" (for true) or "F" (for false).

1. T   F   At times I feel as if God does not give His full attention to the details of my life.

2. T   F   When I need God it sometimes seems as if He is not helping me very much.

3. T   F   Sometimes I feel as if God has withheld something good from me.

4. T   F   At times I feel as if God may not have a high regard for me.

5. T   F   Sometimes I feel as if God is distant and removed from me.

6. T   F   If God wanted me to do something I did not want to do I might feel as if He was trying to talk me into doing it.

7. T   F   To get God to do something for me, I might feel as if I have to do something for Him.

8. T   F   I feel as if I need to measure up to God's expectations in order to please Him.

9. T   F   When I confess my sin I do not always feel forgiven by God.

10. T   F   There are times when I feel as though I have not gotten a fair deal from God.

11. T   F   If I were in a threatening situation I might not feel God protecting me.

12. T   F   I sometimes feel that God lacks confidence in my ability to accomplish significant things.

13. T   F   I do not always feel sure that God has a special and unique purpose for my life.

14. T   F   When I really need God I sometimes feel as if He has left me on my own.

15. T   F   When I have a decision to make I do not always feel that God is interested in helping me.

16. T   F   Sometimes it seems as if God is not actively involved in helping me with my problems.

17. T   F   I sometimes feel as if God does not want to give me what I need.

18. T   F   At times I feel as if God disapproves of me.

19. T   F   Sometimes I feel as if God is far from me.

20. T   F   Every once in awhile I feel as if God is trying to push me to do something before I am ready.

21. T   F   If I want God's favor I sometimes feel as if I need to earn it.

22. T   F   At times I feel I must push myself to meet God's high demands for me.

23. T   F   When I fail spiritually I sometimes feel as if God is upset with me.

24. T   F   Sometimes it feels as if God judges me harshly.

25. T   F   I don't always feel as if God is there to protect me when someone tries to take advantage of me.

26. T   F   Sometimes I feel as if God doesn't trust me to do important things for Him.

27. T   F   I have the feeling that God's plans for my future may not be very special.

28. T   F   In difficult situations I sometimes do not feel God at my side, helping me and guiding me.

WHEN GOD GETS
HOOKED TO THE PAIN

Scoring

On the chart below, circle the number of each question for which you answered "true." Give yourself 1 point for each "true" answer and 0 points for each "false" answer. For example,

Question #		Score	View of God
(1)	15	_1_	Patient
2	16	_0_	Actively helping
(3)	(17)	_2_	Nurturing

Question #		Score	View of God
1	15	_____	Patient
2	16	_____	Actively helping
3	17	_____	Nurturing
4	18	_____	Encouraging
5	19	_____	Personal and intimate
6	20	_____	Gentle, not controlling
7	21	_____	Unconditionally loving
8	22	_____	Accepting
9	23	_____	Merciful and forgiving
10	24	_____	Fair
11	25	_____	Protecting
12	26	_____	Respectful
13	27	_____	Hopeful
14	28	_____	Faithful

Interpreting

The categories in which you scored two points reveal the aspects of God's character that you have the most difficulty experiencing. These are your trouble spots, your areas of distortion. For example, if you answered "true" on questions eleven and twenty-five, you probably have a hard time feeling that God is protecting you. You may believe it intellectually, but because of your history you have difficulty trusting Him to protect you. Most people have a number of areas of distortion, so don't be surprised if you have many.

The following chart explains how these distortions may have developed and what messages you may believe and live by because of them. For example, if you scored two points on "Actively helping," this is an aspect of God's love that you have a hard time experiencing. Find "Actively helping" on the chart and then read down the column. Do this with each of the characteristics you scored two points on.

	1	**2**	**3**
The truth about God is that He is . . .	Patient	Actively Helping	Nurturing
But we have experienced people who are . . .	Preoccupied, dismissing, impatient	Unconcerned, uninvolved, unkind, non-nurturing	Begrudging, stingy, withholding
Because of these experiences, we may live by the message that . . .	"I'm neglected and forgotten by others."	"I don't get any help. I have to take care of myself."	"I must get all I can and hang on to it."
And we may have unconsciously come to fear / expect that God is like them. Perhaps He too is . . .	Preoccupied	Uninvolved	Withholding

4	5	6	7
Encouraging	Personal & Intimate	Gentle / Not Controlling	Unconditionally loving
Criticizing, condemning, disapproving, belittling	Distant, aloof, untouchable, inaccessible, fake	Pushy, manipulative, cajoling, exploiting, rude, harsh	Conditional, contingent
"I always get put down."	"I get excluded and left out."	"I'm tired of being pushed around and forced into things."	"I have to be in control to get what I want."
Shaming	Inaccessible	Manipulating	Conditional

	8	**9**	**10**
The truth about God is that He is . . .	Accepting	Merciful, forgiving	Fair
But we have experienced people who are . . .	Imposing, expecting, insisting, demanding	Perfectionistic, unrelenting	Partial, unfair, unjust, unreasonable
Because of these experiences, we may live by the message that . . .	"I must achieve bigger and better things."	"I have to be perfect and make my world perfect."	"I don't get treated fairly."
And subconsciously we may have come to fear / expect that God is like them. Perhaps He too is . . .	Demanding	Perfectionistic	Partial

11	12	13	14
Protecting	Respectful	Hopeful	Faithful
Passive, weak, unprotective, impotent	Rejecting, critical, judging, sarcastic	Despairing, negative, pessimistic	Inconsistent, abandoning, untrustworthy, unfaithful
"I'm vulnerable to being hurt. I must protect myself."	"I'm not believed in or respected."	"I don't have hope. Things don't work out for me."	"I can't count on anyone or I'll be let down."
Passive	Rejecting	Hopeless	Abandoning

The following responses are from women who have worked through this questionnaire and have attempted to understand the barriers that keep them from experiencing more of God. I've asked them to tell their stories and relate their feelings or fears about Him. What they describe will help you understand how your "painful places" may be affecting your own relationship with God. Even with sound theology in our heads, we will fear rejection and abandonment if in our hearts God is hooked to the pain.

You may want to go first to the descriptions that match the aspects of God you have a hard time experiencing. Then read the others to see if some of them fit as well.

1. PATIENT VS. PREOCCUPIED
Message: "I'm neglected and forgotten by others."

My parents were always very busy with church, attending meetings and running programs. They never had much time for me. I felt guilty about wanting their attention because they were doing important things. I saw myself as a bother to them. We rarely talked about how we were doing or what was going on in our lives. Feelings were totally ignored. We were supposed to be self-controlled and to spend our energies on whatever needed to be done at the church. So I learned to forget about my needs and focus on others. Now, as an adult, I find myself busy doing ministry too. It's not that I don't enjoy the things I do for the church, it's just that I recognize that I ignore other important things in my life because I don't know how to face them. I know how to do "ministry" and take care of others, but I'm not always sure how to connect with my own kids. Somehow, meeting the needs of "others" doesn't include my family. I feel irritated when they want more

from me. I realize that I am preoccupied in the same way my parents were and that I am communicating to my children that their needs are not important to me.

I'm afraid that God feels the same way about me. I worry that my concerns are foolish, that He thinks I should just be grateful for what I have and get on with the business of taking care of things. When I pray, I guess I don't really expect an answer. I feel silly for asking for His attention when my needs are so small in the big picture. It's just an exercise to make me feel as if I've at least tried to get His help. If I were really in trouble I think He'd be there for me, but in the day-to-day stuff I think He expects me to handle it on my own.

Write about relationships you've had that were similar to this.

Write about how you relate to this message.

Write about how this affects your relationship with God.

2. Actively Helping vs. Uninvolved
Message: "I don't get any help. I have to take care of myself."

I've been basically on my own since I was little. My brothers and I got very little help or encouragement from my parents. As long as we were busy, that's all they cared about. I learned to take care of myself. Now I don't want to be a burden to anyone. When people offer to help me with something I say, "No, that's okay," because I don't want to bother them. I don't expect anyone to take care of me. I'm the only one I can count on. But I notice that I get angry and resentful because there's no one to nurture me. I give and give with little recognition. People just expect me to take care of things.

I feel this anger a lot in my marriage. I married someone who doesn't pay much attention to me. I feel as if I'm always thinking about how I can make his life easier but he's never thinking about my needs. He sends me the same message—that I'm on my own.

I have those feelings in my relationship with God. I think He wants me to take care of things myself. I know He loves me, but I don't think of Him as interested in the details of my life. I've always felt as if He was there for me, but I don't want to be a burden or a bother to Him. If I asked for something, He would probably answer but I don't think He really wants to be that involved. I don't expect Him to take care of me. If I have desires, it's my job to get them fulfilled. My happiness is up to me.

WHEN GOD GETS
HOOKED TO THE PAIN

Write about relationships you've had that were similar to this.

Write about how you relate to this message.

Write about how this affects your relationship with God.

3. NURTURING VS. WITHHOLDING
Message: "I must get all I can and hang on to it."

Appearances were everything in my family. Things needed to be just so. The house, the car, the clothes. There was a big focus on physical appearance. The outfit had to be just perfect or it was not good enough. I needed to have matching socks, shoes, and hair accessories—from head to foot, everything had to be

just right. And to make the package complete, I was supposed to be perfect academically, socially, and spiritually. My mother believed that having a perfect appearance was the way to earn love. I learned to believe that too. Outside I had it all "together," but inside I was empty. She gave me lots of material things but withheld what I really needed. My parents divorced by the time I was seven, and my father withdrew emotionally. There was no way to fill up the hole inside.

By the time I was in eighth grade I was using drugs to cope. I remember going to school one day totally high and everyone knew it. I got in big trouble. I freaked out and had a panic attack. My mom didn't know what to do with me. She made attempts to get me some help, but the biggest thing I remember is that when I went back to school I had a brand new outfit. That was her way of fixing things. There was a lot of shopping after a crisis. She would say, "We need to fix that," then she would buy a lot of stuff to make it right.

The emptiness is still there. So I shop and eat to fill it. I know that it won't complete me, but I feel a little better after I get all the things on my list. When I don't have enough money to buy all the pieces to an outfit for me or for the kids, I feel shame. Then I use food. Food is so tangible and available. I keep using it because I don't have much of the other stuff I want in my life.

I don't feel as if I have what I need from God either. I'm afraid to go to Him until I get everything just right. Then I expect Him to withhold help from me or to bless somebody else rather than me because I haven't done well enough. My reaction is to withhold myself from Him to avoid feeling disappointed when He doesn't nurture me. I don't trust Him to give me what I need, so I have to get it for myself.

Write about relationships you've had that were similar to this.

_____

_____

Write about how you relate to this message.

_____

_____

_____

Write about how this affects your relationship with God.

_____

_____

_____

4. ENCOURAGING VS. SHAMING
Message: "I always get put down."

My mother was always critical of my appearance. Although loving in many ways, she never seemed satisfied with the way I looked—not enough make-up or the wrong color clothing for my complexion, my dress was too short or too long, my hair style too unkempt, etc. On the day of my university graduation, her first words to me were, "You're not wearing enough make-up. You really should look your best on this day."

I watch myself pass on this message to my daughter. My daughter is a bit heavy for her age. I'm often reminding her to choose something better to eat or telling her she doesn't need more dessert. I work on that daily but deep down I believe that glamorous, more attractive people are better off. I see myself subtly putting her down because she doesn't look as good as she could. I fool myself into believing that I am teaching her to take care of herself, but it's still a message of conditional love: "I'll love you more if you are thinner."

My relationship with God is confused by a perception that He is critical too. My fear is that His blessings will come only if I achieve a perfect Christian life—pray correctly, study intently, serve continuously. If things go wrong I assume that God is letting me know I am not good enough in some way.

Write about relationships you've had that were similar to this.

_____

_____

_____

Write about how you relate to this message.

_____

_____

_____

Write about how this affects your relationship with God.

_____

_____

_____

5. Personal and Intimate vs. Inaccessible
Message: "I get excluded and left out."

I was twelve years old when my dad left and took my brothers with him. My mom went to work, and I was left alone. Suddenly, I wasn't a part of anything bigger than myself. I often wondered why they didn't care enough to make it work. What was wrong with me? Why wasn't I good enough to stay for? I worried that I had contributed to the break-up. If I had been a better child, maybe they would they have stayed together. That time in my life taught me not to trust anyone because I knew he or she would leave me. I still miss my dad and wish he was more a part of my life, but he rarely calls me. He just doesn't want to be there for me.

Now I always worry about being excluded by others. I'm paranoid about being left out.

Even though I have a lot of relationships, I'm afraid that people are only with me because they have to be, or because they feel sorry for me. Even in my marriage, I've been plagued by this belief that I'm not good enough for the relationship. I've been testing it from the beginning. Sometimes consciously, sometimes subconsciously. I hear myself telling him that I'm not right for him, that I don't deserve him. Sometimes I'll say something inappropriate or unkind and then say, "See, you deserve someone better than me." I was sure that at some point I would do something that would cause him to reject me. I even became involved in an affair at one point. When I look back at that now, I can see that I was trying to ruin this good thing that God had given me. It was too scary waiting for him to

reject me, so I tried to bring on the inevitable. But he's stayed with me, forcing me to believe in his love for me.

I have a hard time accepting that God wants to be personal and intimate with me. I can believe that He loves me because I'm His child and that He needs me to participate in building His kingdom, but He feels very far off. I struggle with believing that He wants to include me in an intimate relationship.

Write about relationships you've had that were similar to this.

_____

_____

_____

Write about how you relate to this message.

_____

_____

_____

Write about how this affects your relationship with God.

_____

_____

6. GENTLE VS. MANIPULATING
Message: "I'm tired of being pushed around and forced into things."

A friend of one of my brothers molested me when I was in junior high. I thought all guys were users so I learned to use that against them. In high school, I started manipulating the guys I became involved with. I learned to make them want me and then refuse to give in to them. I remained a virgin more out of a desire to control them than because of my morality.

Being manipulative was a family trait. There were lots expectations that had to be met or else. There was a lot of harsh treatment when I didn't do things right—yelling, throwing things, slapping. No one was interested in how I felt or what was going on in my life. I know that I treat others the same way. I'm impatient and unkind sometimes. I would never describe myself as gentle.

It's hard to relate to the idea of God being gentle. When I am struggling with sin, I fear that God will deal with me harshly. I expect Him to send people into my life to cut me down to size or reprimand me. Even when I feel as if I am growing, there's still an expectation that God is unhappy and will let me know through someone's criticism that I'm not making enough progress. Not only am I afraid to tell people when I am struggling, I'm afraid to tell people when I think I'm doing well! I always have my guard up.

Write about relationships you've had that were similar to this.

Write about how you relate to this message.

_____

_____

_____

Write about how this affects your relationship with God.

_____

_____

_____

7. Unconditionally Loving vs. Conditional
Message: "I have to be in control to get what I want."

During most of my childhood, my older brother molested me. Despite his abuse, I adored him. He gave me special attention and protected me from other kids. I thought that he really loved me. But when I eventually refused to let him touch me anymore, he totally rejected me. He had controlled our whole relationship and had always been able to get what he wanted. When he could no longer do that, he wanted nothing to do with me. I decided then that I would never be at the mercy of anyone else. I became determined to control relationships so I would

WHEN GOD GETS
HOOKED TO THE PAIN

1 0 8

be safe. Everyone I chose to be involved with was submissive. I picked weak boyfriends who would let me control them. I needed to be the one who had the power in the relationship. When I'm not in a one-up position, I feel anxious about being rejected.

I am even afraid to give up control to God. I'm afraid He'll let something bad happen. I don't think that He wants bad things to happen to me, I just don't believe He'll make sure they don't. If I'm in control, I feel like I have a better chance of making sure things go the way I want. I'm too afraid to rely on God or someone else for my well-being.

Write about relationships you've had that were similar to this.

_____

_____

_____

Write about how you relate to this message.

_____

_____

_____

Write about how this affects your relationship with God.

WHEN GOD GETS
HOOKED TO THE PAIN

_____

_____

_____

8. ACCEPTING VS. DEMANDING
Message: "I must achieve bigger and better things."

My family was impossible to please. My grandmothers were constantly critical. They both had huge expectations of me. They were definite about what I should do with my life. When I didn't do things the way they wanted me to, they saw me as a failure. They'd say, "You're really blowing it. You're turning out just like your mother." My parents were the same way. They never gave strokes for anything. I was doing all these things but they never validated my achievements. The things I accomplished were either not done as well as they should have been or were not significant enough to deserve recognition.

My religious training in Catholic school led me to believe that God was like the nuns who always told me that I didn't measure up. I looked up to them and they made me feel awful, like a guilty person always needing to go to confession. Even now, after years of being a Christian, I feel as if God is shaking His head and wondering when I am going to shape up. I keep trying to find a way to earn His love and acceptance. I've done tons of ministry, tons of quiet time materials and Bible studies. I try to live without sin, but I feel as if all my efforts are never enough. I'm constantly setting goals and trying to do what's right but I'm always feeling like a failure.

Write about relationships you've had that were similar to this.

_____

_____

_____

Write about how you relate to this message.

_____

_____

_____

Write about how this affects your relationship with God.

_____

_____

_____

9. MERCIFUL VS. PERFECTIONISTIC
Message: "I have to be perfect and make my world perfect."

I was raised in a conservative Baptist community in the south. The whole culture taught that there is a perfect way to be a proper Christian young lady. I was always expected to perform at my best—to be spiritual, to be a good daughter, to follow the rules. There was no room to fail. If I was capable of doing something, I needed to do it and do it well. Being average was not accept-

able. There was always someone there making sure I didn't fall outside the guidelines.

I still try to do things perfectly, to make sure everything is just right—that the tennis shoes are white, that the silverware is stacked in the drawer, that the anger doesn't go over the top, that I never roll my eyes in disgust, that we are on time no matter what, that we appear put together.

I have this perception that God expects perfection from me too. I have to be perfect to be worthy of His love. I have to excel in everything I am capable of doing because being average is not good enough for God either. When I am imperfect in my own eyes it's as if I hear God saying, "Why didn't you get an A+ if you were capable of it?" I'm afraid to stand before Him because I haven't "arrived" yet. I'm so afraid He is disappointed in me.

Write about relationships you've had that were similar to this.

_____

_____

_____

Write about how you relate to this message.

_____

_____

_____

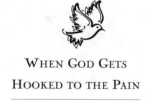

Write about how this affects your relationship with God.

_____

_____

_____

10. FAIR VS. PARTIAL
Message: "I don't get treated fairly."

In our church youth group I got labeled as a troublemaker. It was true that I didn't always follow all the rules but anytime there was a problem, I was the first person they suspected. Eventually, I was asked to leave the group for something I didn't have anything to do with. They just assumed it was me and wouldn't believe me when I told them it wasn't. It still makes me mad when I think about it. They rejected me unfairly and failed to understand that as a new Christian I needed a chance to grow.

I feel unfairly judged a lot in my marriage too. When we are in conflict my husband accuses me of not caring or not trying to make our marriage work. My reaction is to withdraw even more. I feel as if I'm doing the best I can but it's never enough. Sometimes I feel like giving up and just being bad since that's how he views me.

I guess I expect God to deal unfairly with me too. I don't expect Him to intervene for me the same way He does for others. For some reason they get something I don't. It seems like He is willing to rescue them but not me. It's hard to understand why He does what He does. So I hold Him at arm's length to try to protect myself from being hurt. Needing Him too much is too big a risk. I want to make sure that I don't become too dependent on Him because He is so unpredictable.

Write about relationships you've had that were similar to this.

_____

_____

_____

Write about how you relate to this message.

_____

_____

_____

Write about how this affects your relationship with God.

_____

_____

_____

11. PROTECTIVE VS. PASSIVE
Message: "I'm vulnerable to being hurt. I must protect myself."

I know my parents loved me but they weren't paying much attention to what was going on in my life. I was molested on and off for many years of my childhood. Whenever I was hurt or afraid and would go to them for help, they would dismiss me. "You're fine," is what they would always say. It was confusing to try to make sense of that as a child. I was supposed to be fine, to be able to handle whatever was happening to me, but I felt terrified and paralyzed so much of the time. I got the message loud and clear that no one was going to rescue me. I would just have to handle the fear myself.

Now as an adult I am vigilant about protecting myself. I get angry when I am placed in situations where I feel afraid. I keep waiting for somebody to show up and rescue me, but it's never going to happen. The other adults in my life are no braver than I am.

I prepare myself to be unprotected by God as well. Even though I ask for His help in scary or overwhelming situations, I don't expect a response from Him. I expect Him to be weak and impotent, just like the people in my life. I assume that He will not move to save me, and that I will have to save myself.

Write about relationships you've had that were similar to this.

Write about how you relate to this message.

Write about how this affects your relationship with God.

12. RESPECTFUL VS. REJECTING
Message: "I'm not believed in or respected."

I wanted to be respected by my dad so badly that I pretended to be another person for him. I knew he wouldn't approve of who I really was so I tried to be the kind of person he would be proud of. Hearing him talk critically about other people let me know what not to be like. He seemed to approve of this person I had made up, so I kept up the act. When I got pregnant and had an abortion, I knew I would have to keep it a secret. I had heard him talk about what losers women were who had abortions. Being around him was miserable because of the fear of being found out.

It's been hard for me to be real with other people in my life. I am afraid that if I stop pretending to be what I am supposed to be, there will be no one there to love me. Withholding the truth of my life seems normal to me. I can avoid being rejected if I can figure out what people want from me.

In my relationship with God this comes up big time. I'm always comparing myself to others to help me figure out if I am valuable to Him. Now that my husband and I are struggling with infertility I feel judged by God, as if He's saying I'm not doing a good enough job with the child I have, so why would He give me

another. I compare myself to women who have more children and try to prove to myself that I don't deserve this judgment from Him, that He made a mistake. Then I try to make myself more valuable to God in hopes that if I am more worthy of His love, maybe He'll remove this judgment from me. I know that none of this is true about God's dealings, but I struggle with these feelings a lot.

Write about relationships you've had that were similar to this.

_____

_____

_____

But you, O Sovereign LORD, deal well with me for your name's sake; out of the goodness of your love, deliver me. For I am poor and needy, and my heart is wounded within me.

Psalm 109:21-22

Write about how you relate to this message.

_____

_____

_____

Write about how this affects your relationship with God.

_____

_____

13. Hopeful vs. Hopeless
Message: "I have no hope. Things don't work out for me."

Things never seemed to work out for our family. My dad became disabled when we were young, and my mom had to support the family. Life was such a struggle for them. Whenever they attempted to pursue a dream they had, things fell apart. They would get excited about some good possibility, but it would never happen. Their dreams never came true. They didn't have hope for themselves, and they passed on that hopelessness to us. My dad especially had low expectations for his life, and for us, and we all met those expectations. We were major low achievers. We never learned to persevere.

I've always dropped out of things. I dropped out of college when I was close to being done and still haven't finished. I guess I don't expect to complete things or be successful so I don't push through things when they get hard. I don't think much about what could be or what I might want for myself. I learned that there's no point in dreaming because things just don't work out.

I don't think of God as having any plans for me. I don't see myself as essential to His work because I don't think I'm capable of contributing in a significant way. I know that I'm good at some things but not at anything that makes a difference in people's lives.

Write about relationships you've had that were similar to this.

Write about how you relate to this message.

_____

_____

_____

Write about how this affects your relationship with God.

_____

_____

_____

14. FAITHFUL VS. ABANDONING
Message: "I can't count on anyone or I'll be disappointed."

When I was a little girl, I adored my daddy. Even when he and my mother divorced, I continued to believe in him. Over time, however, I began to see how selfish he was. First he was hours late for visits with me, then days. Eventually he didn't even show up on the weekends he had promised to spend with me. It was painful to realize that I had given him my heart and it was of no value to him.

I've had the same experience in my marriage. When my husband and I were

dating, we broke up because he was unfaithful to me. I was done with the relationship, but he continued to pursue me. As time went by I began to feel God changing my heart toward him. After several years of marriage I found out that he was having an affair and struggling with a sexual addiction. I felt like God had set me up. He knew that this man would betray me but He had encouraged me to open up to him again and allowed me to marry him. I felt fooled. I had given my heart again to someone who was untrustworthy.

I am so afraid that God really can't be trusted. Intellectually, I know that's not true, but I can't seem to get past the fear that really giving myself to Him means I'm in for more betrayal. I don't know how to believe that my needs are important to Him. I feel as if our relationship is about me doing what He wants me to do but I don't expect Him to take care of me in a way that makes me feel safe and valued.

Write about relationships you've had that were similar to this.

_____

_____

_____

Write about how you relate to this message.

_____

_____

_____

Write about how this affects your relationship with God.

_____

_____

_____

Caroline's Story

July 1994

As I prepare to go to my high school reunion, these feelings come up related to the abortion. Anything associated with that time triggers these feelings. I'd give anything to push them aside and go back to pretending it never happened. But it's too late. I have begun to tell the truth about who I really am.

I went through old memorabilia today and found the actual list he and I made of the pros and cons of keeping the baby. It made me sick to my stomach to read some of the letters between us about what choice we should make. I was so shocked to see that we really felt that God was in our lives. If we really knew Him, how could we have made such an awful choice? I discussed this with my group and

they helped me put into perspective that I was not the person then that I am today. I was 17! My family was totally messed up. My dad was a drug addict. My mom went from relationship to relationship and condoned my sexual behavior. The person making that choice was not the person I am today. That had a big impact on me. Not that I can completely forgive myself, but it helped to put into perspective how young and alone I was then. Lord, why can't I forgive myself? Why do I feel forgiveness for a while and then the shame wells up inside me and I feel like a worthless mess again? Why, when I know intellectually that you died for this sin, does it seem somehow too big for you to forgive?

December 1995

Went to a funeral today for a friend whose baby was born dead. I feel unworthy of all the blessings I have in my life. I really don't understand how You could love me if I did such a terrible thing. I keep waiting for You to punish me, to make me somehow pay for my sin. I wait for it but You just keep blessing me. This is very frustrating because a part of me continues to wonder when my time is going to be up. I wonder if I'm going to keep being tortured with more and more blessings and then a REALLY BIG punishment is going to come. As others around me deal with pain, loss, and grief, my life continues to get better, more full, packed with love and life. How is this fair when they haven't committed this sin? I kept thinking, "This next baby will have something wrong with it, or my husband will be taken away, or something horrible will happen to my other children." When our third baby was born totally healthy, I was shocked. Obviously relieved. But then guilty. It's as if I'm wishing that I could just pay my dues, have some-

thing tragic happen, and get it over with. You are showing me that that's not how you work at all. You have shown me that it's not about penance. It's about embracing this pain, being unafraid to admit this is part of my life. Through sharing the depths of my heart with others I have found a freedom, and the truth of You has become more clear in the process. As I've revealed more, those I love haven't rejected me. Instead, they love me more and feel more connected to me. I, in turn, feel more connected to them. Not as alone, not as insecure. I have begun to realize that this pain is not one that is going to immediately go away. It is part of my life. As I talk about it more I learn more about You and discover the truth of your character — that you will not pull the rug out from under me at any minute.

Certainly bad things may come my way over the course of time, but they won't be "pay back" for my bad choices. As I think about this I get a glimpse of peace. I realize that You are speaking to me through these conversations in my head. I get glimpses of relief, the feeling of being treasured, of being guilt-free. I am beginning to believe that you still have a plan for my life, that I didn't destroy your plan, that you can work despite my bad choice.

Write about any thoughts or feelings you have after reading Caroline's story.

_____

_____

_____

WHEN GOD GETS
HOOKED TO THE PAIN

Afraid...
I tremble at the thought
My walls are up.
They keep me safe.
But it's so lonely inside.
I know you want my heart
but I'm afraid to give it.
What will you do to it?
What will I have to face to get where you're taking me?
How can I? Yet I know I can.
You are so big, so mighty,
You love me so deeply that you are willing to go slow.
Go gentle.
Show me, reveal to me
what I need to know.
I'm afraid.
I need your comfort,
your assurance,
that I will see the dawn.

—Kathy Escobar

Write to God about your desires to experience Him more fully. Tell Him about your longings to feel His protection and to rest in His love, faithfulness, and acceptance.

_____

_____

_____

_____

_____

_____

_____

_____

_____

_____

7 When the Pain Slips into Relationships

Right Feeling, Wrong Target

MY DAUGHTER Katie is sitting on the floor in the hallway with her brother Joshua. She is four; he is almost two. Josh whacks her; she cries. He whacks her again; she just sits and cries. At first I am annoyed. I tell her to move away from him. She doesn't. He hits her again. She sits and cries. My annoyance builds. My stomach tightens. I breathe faster. I begin screaming, "Get up and run away from him! You're not helpless! Stop acting like you're helpless!"

I tell myself that I am upset because she will not protect herself and because it's important for her to learn that she is not powerless. But the truth is, I am screaming at her because I was once powerless, and I am angry at myself. Angry because I never fought back, never told on him, never screamed at him, "Leave me alone. I'm just a little girl!"

Today I am screaming, but I am screaming at the wrong person.

I will take refuge in the shadow of your wings until the disaster has passed.

Psalm 57:1

It happens so fast. Something in my life today taps into pain from long ago and suddenly I am making people in the present pay for things done to me by people in my past. Those people got away with hurting me. These people will not. I didn't know then how to protect myself, but I do now. And so I blame and attack or withdraw and push away with the force of thirty years of unresolved feelings.

This is not working.

My friend Judy says it's hard to love people who are stuck in painful places. She says they are like broken cups. It doesn't matter how much you pour into them, you can never fill them up. I have been a person who could not be filled up, expecting the people in my life to be more than they could possibly be.

When I married, I was in love. I thought I was in love with my husband. But it turns out that I was in love with the way he made me feel. He was confident, exciting, and passionate about me— everything I wanted in a husband. When I was with him, I felt smart, funny, and desirable. I felt taken care of, cherished. I believed, as many brides do, that he would make everything better. He would fill up the empty places inside of me. I would never be lonely or afraid again because I had him. God had sent my Prince Charming, and he would fix everything!

But "Cinderella" is only a fairy tale, and Prince Charming had powers that no mortal man can muster.

Not many months after we were married, I stopped feeling "in love." My husband didn't need me the way I needed him. I thought something was wrong with him so I tried to fix him. That frustrated both of us. He kept saying, "No matter what I do, it's never enough for you." I kept hearing, "I don't love you enough to give you what you need." I had no idea that I needed so much more than he was capable of giving, more than anyone could have given me. I vacillated between feeling hopeless and angry—until I discovered that the pain was not all about him.

As I have worked with groups of women the past few years, I have observed similar thinking patterns in them. We all have the sense that our relationships ought to be more fulfilling, that we ought to feel more whole, but we don't know how to make it happen. We crave connection and at the same time are afraid to pursue it.

Here's my little theory about women and intimacy (I think it is likely true for men too, but I won't speak for them).

We want and need intimacy	*but . . .*	we are afraid of intimacy
We become angry, depressed, anxious when we don't experience intimacy	*but . . .*	we guard against or sabotage intimacy by . . . • *using blame and defensiveness, which push others away.* • *being busy, moving fast, staying focused on getting things done, achieving more.* • *"hiding out," focusing on what's wrong with our bodies to avoid physical intimacy.*

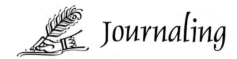 # Journaling

We are aware that our needs are unmet, but we are unaware of the ways in which we are responsible for our isolation. We know something needs to change, but we think the something is "them." So we attack the problem by attacking them. When that doesn't work, instead of trying a different approach, we intensify our attempts to change the other person.

Think about yourself in relationships to significant people (e.g., wife to husband; daughter to mother / father; mother to daughter / son; friend to friend) as you answer the following questions:

In what ways is the relationship unfulfilling or painful? What is missing? What is causing the pain?

_____

_____

_____

_____

_____

Who am I trying the hardest to change? What is he or she doing or not doing that I wish were different?

_____

_____

_____

_____

_____

How do I usually feel after interactions with this person?

_____

_____

_____

_____

_____

What needs of my own am I trying to meet in this relationship?

_____

_____

_____

_____

_____

How do I feel about getting closer to this person? In what way do I guard against intimacy?

_____

_____

_____

_____

_____

Relationships become painful when needs go unrecognized and unmet. Conflict often occurs not because people disagree about where to go for dinner or who should do the dishes, but because underlying issues are not addressed. Conversations about daily tasks and decisions escalate into arguments because partners feel as if their needs are not considered or their feelings are not validated. All of us have been involved in conflict over small issues—like whose job it is to take out the trash or who should put the kids to bed—that somehow became knock-down, drag-outs, causing tension for days or weeks. How does that happen?

Conflict escalates when a situation in the present triggers feelings that are still unresolved from our past. Those unresolved feelings may be from experiences with that person over time, others in our past, or our family of origin. A psychologist friend of mine says she believes that conflicts are generally made up of 20 percent current stuff and 80 percent past stuff! Making connections between our feelings in the present and our experiences in the past can help us stop conflicts from getting out of control and get our relationships moving again.

The following chart shows how conflicts escalate in relationships. This pattern of escalation tends to happen over and over in many relationships, with no resolution occuring. Instead we find ways to ignore it or patch it up and go on, only to end up in trouble again. Each situation adds fuel to the fire of our negative beliefs. Read the chart from the bottom up, starting with "current situation."

ESCALATION OF CONFLICT

REINFORCEMENT
Believing that the current situation / relationship is solely responsible for the intensity further escalates the conflict. Anxiety and anger build. These same feelings will resurface with another trigger situation.

RESPONSE
Your partner will likely be unable or unwilling to validate your feelings because he will feel the need to protect himself from your BIG reaction. He may defend himself by attacking, ignoring, withdrawing, etc. Feelings that go unheard, unvalidated, and unexplored further intensify the conflict.

REACTION
Based on the BIG feelings being experienced. May be expressed as displaced or disproportionate anger.

DISPLACED ANGER
Anger is detoured from one person or experience to another.

DISPROPORTIONATE ANGER
Anger is experienced with more intensity than the situation warrants.

TRIGGER
This situation ignites unresolved feelings from the past, creating BIG feelings that are disproportionate to the present circumstance.

CURRENT SITUATION

REINFORCEMENT

Because he will not agree to buy the door and withdraws from me, my feelings intensify. My belief that I am all on my own and that no one loves me enough to protect me is reinforced when there is no resolution to the problem. I am now further convinced that he cannot be trusted to protect me.

I am stuck. I believe that my big feelings are all about this current situation. This cuts me off from exploring why I am so upset and what can be done to bring resolution.

RESPONSE

Ken doesn't understand why I am so upset about a security door and why I am questioning his love for me. He says it is not fair for me to say he doesn't care and will not protect me. He still does not want a security door. My anger is so big that he feels the need to protect himself and so he withdraws from me.

REACTION

My feelings get bigger as I try to express how important this is to me. "I need to feel safe. Why don't you care if I feel unprotected?"

DISPLACED ANGER

I felt unprotected in my family of origin. My fears were dismissed as silly or unimportant. I am angry about how it was then but I am unaware of that, so I dump all my anger.

TRIGGER

I feel angry because I hear Ken say my fears are silly.

DISPROPORTIONATE ANGER

It is reasonable for a person to feel as Ken does about security doors. And it is reasonable to have a discussion about what other options might make me feel safe. But I feel so angry that I cannot consider his feelings or express my own feelings without attacking his.

CURRENT SITUATION

I explain to Ken that I want a security door on the front door. Salespeople (mostly men) come to the door and I feel vulnerable. Ken tells me he doesn't like security doors because they make a house seem less welcoming and he doesn't think one is necessary.

WHEN THE PAIN SLIPS
INTO RELATIONSHIPS

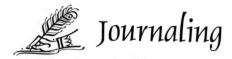 # Journaling

Which relationships do you often experience conflict in? What are the conflicts generally about?

_____

_____

_____

_____

Write about your most recent conflict in an important relationship. What happened? How did you feel? What did both of you say? How did the conflict end?

_____

_____

_____

_____

_____

In what past situations or relationships do you remember having the same feelings?

_____

_____

_____

_____

_____

_____

POWERFUL BUT REJECTING	VULNERABLE BUT INVITING
"You never make time for us to be together. You don't care about our relationship."	"I'm feeling anxious and insecure. I'm worried that you are pulling away from me."

REVEALER	RECEIVER

This is your turn to talk. Your job is to take a risk, to reveal more of yourself, to discover more of yourself.

This is your turn to hear. Your job is to listen and understand, to ask questions, to try to connect to your partner's feelings.

FOCUS

Talk only about one issue. Before you begin, make sure you are clear about what issue it is you want to talk about.

EXPRESS

Talk about your feelings. Blaming, accusing, or name-calling will prevent your partner from hearing you.

Remind yourself that this is about you and a problem you are having. Focus on explaining the feelings rather than the situation which aroused them.

DISCOVER

Be open to self-discovery. Look for the feelings buried beneath your initial or obvious feeling (e.g., your initial feeling is anger but underneath you feel abandoned; your initial feeling is defensiveness but underneath you feel ashamed).

Ask yourself, "When in the past have I felt this way?" "What other situations make me feel this way?" "What other situations make me feel this way?" "Is it possible that this present situation is tapping into feelings from the past?"

SEPARATE

Your partner is a separate person with his / her own feelings, perspective, and history.

Remind yourself, "I do not own this problem. I do not need to take this personally. I do not need to get upset and I do not need to fix this problem."

Don't defend yourself, argue, or cross-complain.

EXPLORE

Ask questions. Think about situations in which you have felt similar feelings. Ask if this is the kind of feeling he / she is talking about.

DISCOVER

Keep exploring until you are clear about what your partner's feelings are. Check out your level of understanding by recapping what you are hearing. Remember that you can increase your partner's desire to hear and understand you by allowing your partner to fully discuss his / her feelings.

WHEN THE PAIN SLIPS
INTO RELATIONSHIPS

A Word about Anger

We frequently miss our underlying or primary emotion because we move quickly from hurt, embarrassment, or abandonment to anger. Anger puts us in control. It gives us power and protects us from feeling more painful feelings. Staying in anger helps us stay in the driver's seat, and that feels good. *But it pushes people away from us, escalating the conflict and preventing us from resolving the problem.*

Resolving conflict requires that we express the emotion underneath the anger. That leaves us vulnerable, without protection, and it feels scary. *But it allows us to move toward the other person, giving us the opportunity to connect and experience intimacy.* Here's an example of what I mean.

The following guidelines will give you some help in expressing (REVEALER) and hearing (RECEIVER) difficult feelings. You may want to practice dealing with a painful issue by role-playing with a friend to prepare you to tackle a real conflict you are struggling with.

 Journaling

I am afraid to let go of self-protection. I must hold back a piece of myself or I will have no control. I will be destroyed if I abandon myself

to really loving, really needing. If I need them, really need them, they will abandon me.

What are you afraid of in your most intimate relationships?

_____

But you are a
shield around me, O
LORD; you bestow
glory on me and
lift up my head.
Psalm 3:3

_____

What do you wish you could feel more of?

_____

_____

_____

_____

_____

8 Learning to Fly

With Wings of Faith, Hope, and Love

To FIND the freedom to fly we must understand and accept our life story. God somehow becomes deeply involved with us when we begin to speak the truth, when we admit how powerless and hopeless we feel, when we tell Him how much we long for deeper intimacy in our relationships.

Doing so opens us up to His power and allows Him to finally address us as whole people. We no longer go to Him with just a part of us—the part that we think is acceptable. We go with all of who we are—our fears, our insecurities, our anger about what He's allowed in our lives, our confusion about what we don't think He's doing enough of. Then we can experience a real relationship, a real conversation.

When we are finally ready to be still and listen, we can begin hearing His voice and feeling His restoring hand at work in us.

Dan Allender talks about this process of healing and finding freedom from the past. He says it involves the growth of faith, hope, and love:

He will cover

you with his feathers,

and under his wings you

will find refuge; his

faithfulness will be your

shield and rampart. You will

not fear the terror of night,

nor the arrow that flies

by day…

Psalm 91:4-5

How do we grow faith, hope, and love?

Faith is confidence in the rescuing power of God. It is grown by memory, by struggling and asking hard questions. David became a man after God's own heart because he was willing to remember and be honest with God about the feelings those memories stirred up. In order to grow faith, we must ask hard questions—God, where were you when . . . why didn't you change what was happening? Those of us who have been abused or neglected or ignored don't want to remember. We want to forget the past and move on. But we cannot grow in faith unless we remember, feel the feelings that need to be felt and ask the questions that need to be asked. Then we can come to the place where Joseph did when he said to his brothers who had sold him into slavery, "You meant it for evil but God meant it for good."

The growing of hope involves owning the dreams of your heart. When we have been hurt, we learn to stop believing in hope, we are afraid to hope because we have been disappointed so many times. We tell ourselves that who we are in our worst moments is all we will ever be. We have lost the ability to hope, to dream. Hope is faith for the future. When we have come to a place where we can really believe in the rescuing power of God over our pasts, we can begin to believe in our futures. Hope is leaning into the future to create what God has given for your creation. The Bible teaches that He is continually at work in us to make us more like Him. So even when our circumstances or relationships are painful or look hopeless, we can be sure that regardless of the outcome, He is going to make it possible to be the work of art we were intended to be.

Growing in love requires learning to let go of self-protection. It means repenting of the clenched fist that says, "I will not be hurt again." Learning to love means opening ourselves to relationships and the pain that will inevitably be part of it.

(Adapted from an address by Dan Allender at the 1997 "Trauma and Sexuality Conference," San Diego, CA. Used by permission.)

 Journaling

What are some hard questions you need to ask God? In what ways have you felt abandoned, betrayed, or ignored by Him? Tell Him everything you feel. He wants you to relate to Him honestly. He can handle your feelings, whatever they are.

_____

_____

_____

_____

_____

_____

_____

_____

_____

_____

_____

_____

What are the painful places you are still afraid to visit? Write a sentence to God about that situation.

_____

_____

_____

_____

Write about the dreams of your heart. What are some of the dreams you have for your future, your family, your marriage, your relationship with God? Spend time thinking about how your life would be different if you had hope that God wanted to do good things for you. Write about what that would be like.

If you feel ready, tell God you want to hear from Him. Be still and listen. Write down anything that comes to your mind

_____

_____

_____

_____

_____

_____

_____

_____

I don't remember what started the argument between Ken and me, or why it went so badly. I just remember feeling completely hopeless when it was over. We had been working hard in counseling, but all of the progress seemed like a lie that day. I was deeply discouraged, feeling foolish for having tried so hard to hang on. I sat at my desk with my calculator, trying to figure out how much money it would take to make it as a single parent. Then I wrote in my journal:

October '96

Lord, I feel lost, angry, betrayed. This feels impossible! What am I supposed to do? There is too much pain. He hasn't made any changes for a long time. He is not safe and I cannot make him safe. I feel beaten up, taken advantage of. Lord, when will you act? I have had enough!

That night I had a class to teach, so I tried to put my feelings aside and concentrate on work. Two days later, a student called to tell me that she had felt the need to pray for me after class that night. Autumn told me that while she was praying, a picture had come into her mind and she wanted to share it with me. This is what she told me.

> You were in a field of mud with the Father. I saw you as a child, in a dress, following behind the Father. The field was dark and there was only enough light to see partially. As He walked before you, His feet made imprints in the mud. You walked behind Him, placing your feet, in white shoes, in the imprints. Because he had gone before you, your white shoes remained spotless. Both of you walked a straight path out of the mud.

> Then the image changed and I saw you as an adult, as you are now. You were under the Father's wing. You looked weary. You were not

standing. You looked as if you had fallen and were struggling to regain your strength. The Lord was renewing you under the shelter of His wings. Then I saw the Lord pour out golden sparkling oil all over you. You were drenched in oil. The oil signifies the healing He is doing in you. As I prayed for the Lord to strengthen you, I saw Him place feathers on your arms. One by one the feathers became wings.

As Autumn talked, I sat on my kitchen floor feeling totally overwhelmed. This was a person I hardly knew, someone who had no idea that God had consistently used the images of mud and flying to urge me to grow. And yet, here was another clear message reminding me to continue to believe in what He had already promised—a restored marriage, healing from past hurts, and freedom from the bondage I had become so comfortable with. The fact that things were still painful and unresolved didn't mean that He had stopped working or that He had forgotten me. He was still doing exactly what He said. It was time for me to stop looking back and believing what had been. It was time to move forward and leave the mud behind.

God is sending messages to you too. I don't know how, but I believe that He is. I don't know what He is saying to you, but I believe that He is speaking to each of us—wooing us out of the mud. And I believe that if we listen and wait, if we invite Him into a deeper relationship, He will come. Some way, somehow, He will respond to your openness. Listen for Him, watch for Him. You may hear something that sounds like His voice in a conversation with a friend, in a dream, in a song you hear on the radio, in something you write in your journal, in something your child says to you, or in a still, small voice. He is there, waiting to connect with you.

When I first began to look at my painful places, I struggled to grow. I longed for more intimacy in my relationships, but I was afraid to believe there was a way to get it. I wasn't sure I deserved to experience freedom or to enjoy my relationships. I had constant fears that this was all a set-up for disappointment. When Ken and I weren't doing well or I was too angry with my kids or I was using food, the Evil One would whisper, "This is who you really are. This is all you ever will be. You cannot fly, you cannot be free. In those moments when you think things are changing, when you feel free and alive, you are only pretending. You are good at pretending."

The voice was so familiar and sounded so true that it was hard not to listen. I wrestled often with that voice. I wrote in my journal . . .

Is it true that I am trying to be more than I am? That I am fooling myself, pursuing something that is not available to me? Or could it be that I am more than my fallenness, that I am most truly, most fully myself in those moments when I *am* flying? When I am living out my giftedness, when I am focused, when I am feeling and loving? Maybe what I am fighting for is the chance to be what I was intended to be!

One day I was greatly encouraged when I came across this from *A God to Call Father* by Michael Phillips:

Those who make sin the foundational starting point for attempting to understand the nature of man do God's creation a grievous wrong. With that sand-built base as their starting point, they are able to understand neither man nor the Father. Rather than undergirding their theologies with the eternal bedrock of Genesis 1—the beginning!—they begin their erroneous expositions at Genesis 3. They come at truth from the wrong angle altogether, thus entirely missing the vital point that goodness lies deeper in the heart of man's nature than the sin, which came later and entered from the outside. *Goodness lies deeper in man because God put himself there. It was very good!* Goodness is intrinsic to man's nature; sin is not. Sin is the corrupting virus that has temporarily contaminated goodness. (Wheaton, IL: Tyndale, 1994, 120).

If we understand that we are image-bearers of the Creator, that we are deeply imprinted with something of Him, we can believe in an escape from painful places. We are not forever trapped by our thinking and behavior patterns. He has created within us the capacity to be more than our experiences have taught us to be. Believing in that capacity is, for me, the hardest part of growth.

When we continue to make mistakes or struggle with issues we thought we had left behind, we are tempted to believe that we have not made any real progress at all. In her book *A Graceful Waiting* Jan Frank explains that we often get discouraged because we think that growth ought to be like climbing the rungs of a ladder. We deal with issues or behaviors on the first rung and then move on to the next rung. When those old issues come up again, we mistakenly assume that we have failed to take any steps. She suggests that growth is more like a spiral. We work on an issue, get some freedom or make some improvement, and work our way up and around the spiral. At some point we will likely hit that same issue again, but it is important to understand that we are hitting it at a higher level. We are not at the same point we were before. We are working at it in a new way, at a new level, to gain deeper healing and restoration in that area.

My mom is a quilter. When she is working on a new quilt, she will show me the pieces and say, "Look at my quilt." She shows me hundreds of small pieces of different colors of fabric and lays them all out on the floor. I squint and try to imagine what it will look like after everything is sewn together and the quilting is done, but I have trouble seeing what she does. She sees what it will be. I see what it is now. She is excited about what it will look like. She doesn't apologize because it isn't really a quilt yet or say that it's probably foolish of her to believe it will be beautiful someday. She calls it a quilt and works continually toward that end, confident that eventually it will be exactly what it was intended to be—a beautiful handmade work of art that will keep her family warm and remind them of her love.

I do the same thing with my life that I do with her quilts. I squint and try to imagine that I can see it as it could be. But too often I let the vision fade with the first mistake. I give up trying because I don't trust that something good could really be accomplished in me. It is much easier to trust her to make quilts. I've

I waited patiently for the LORD; he turned to me and heard my cry. He lifted me out of the slimy pit, out of the mud and mire; he set my feet on a rock and gave me a firm place to stand. He put a new song in my mouth, a hymn of praise to our God. Many will see and fear and put their trust in the LORD.

Psalm 40:1-3

seen her do it over and over—take scraps of material that anyone else would throw away and make something amazing from them.

Trusting God to make something out of me has been much more difficult. But little by little, I have begun to believe that God wants to make a work of art out of me. He invites me to trust Him and to fly! There is nothing I can do to earn His love or make myself deserving; there are no hoops to jump through. I don't have to be somebody special with lots of talent who can change the world. He simply loves me and wants to restore His image in me. He delights in me because I am His little girl. And I am learning that I can be more comfortable in His arms than any-where else.

For me, there have been two questions to settle: One, do I believe that God is inviting me to leave the mud and learn to fly? Two, do I have the courage to go with Him?

It is so much easier to stay in the mud. So much easier to settle for what is familiar. Flying demands so much—constant self-evaluation, feeling, remem-bering, taking responsibility for the way I relate to oth-ers when I hurt them, moving toward others even when I am terrified, trying again even after repeated failures. It is painful, it is overwhelming, and there are lots of set-backs.

There are still a lot of days when I don't want to fly. When I want to say, "Things are so much better than they used to be,

Lord. This is enough freedom for me. I am tired of feeling, tired of trying to make choices that feel so unnatural to me. Let's call it a day."

But the freedom, peace, and wholeness are well worth it. There are moments in my life now that are more precious than I could have imagined. They may look like nothing special to anyone else, but they make me aware that I can feel my whole life! I can lay on my bed with Ken and Katie and Josh and giggle! I can look into their eyes and embrace the deep satisfaction of real connection. I can feel their love and they can feel mine. And we can find our way back to each other when things get ugly. I can cry with my friends and feel strengthened, not pitied. I can know that my failures and weaknesses won't scare them away. I can trust that when I hurt them, they will still love me. I can need them and be needed right back. Best of all, I can feel my relationship with God. I can run to Him when things are falling apart and really believe He will rescue me. I can ask for direction and hear His answer. I can see His restoring hand at work, hear Him cheer me on and know, not just hope or try to believe, but finally *know*, that He can be trusted. It doesn't get any better than that!

Recommended Reading

Allender, Dan. *The Wounded Heart.* Colorado Springs: NavPress, 1995.

Carder, Dave, and Earl Henslin, John Townsend, Henry Cloud, Al Brawand. *Secrets of Your Family Tree.* Chicago: Moody Press, 1991.

Curtis, Brent, and John Eldredge. *The Sacred Romance.* Nashville: Thomas Nelson, 1997.

Frank, Jan. *Door of Hope.* Nashville: Thomas Nelson, 1995.

————. *When Victims Marry.* Nashville: Thomas Nelson, 1990.

Gaultiere, William, and Kristie Gaultiere. *Returning to the Father.* Chicago: Moody Press, 1993.

Halliday, Arthur W., and Judy Wardell Halliday. *Silent Hunger.* Grand Rapids: Revell, 1994.

Blackaby, Henry T., and Claude V. King, *Experiencing God.* Nashville: Broadman & Holman, 1994.

Manning, Brennan. *Abba's Child.* Colorado Springs: NavPress, 1994.

Reinicke, Melinda. *Parables for Personal Growth.* San Diego: Recovery Publishing, 1993.

VanVonderen, Jeff. *Tired of Trying to Measure Up.* Minneapolis: Bethany House, 1989.

Note to the Reader

The publisher invites you to share your response to the message of this book by writing Discovery House Publishers, Box 3566, Grand Rapids, MI 49501, USA. For information about other Discovery House books, music, or videos, contact us at the same address or call 1-800-653-8333. Find us on the Internet at http://www.dhp.org/ or send e-mail to books@dhp.org.